PRENTICE HALL

WORLD HISTORY
THE MODERN ERA

AYP Monitoring
Assessments

PEARSON

Prentice
Hall

Boston, Massachusetts
Upper Saddle River, New Jersey

Boston, Massachusetts
Upper Saddle River, New Jersey

ISBN 0-13-129980-8

2 3 4 5 6 7 8 9 10   09 08 07

Contents

How to Use This Book

AYP Monitoring Assessments provides a clear path to *adequate yearly progress* through systematic testing and recommendations for remediation. Progress monitoring at regular intervals ensures that students understand key content before moving on in the course. With the results of these tests, you will know when to modify instruction because a class is having difficulty and when to assign remediation because individual students need more help.

Beginning the Year: Establishing the Baseline

Teaching for adequate yearly progress (AYP) begins with evaluating student strengths and weaknesses. Before launching into the curriculum, you need to know how well your students read and how proficient they are in social studies skills. Use the following tests to measure student readiness for your course.

Reading Screening Test (pages vi–5)

Administer the Reading Screening Test to evaluate students' ability to read the textbook. This test identifies students who are reading two or more years below grade level. You may wish to consider placing them in intensive intervention, or you may consider having these students use the *Adapted Reading and Note Taking Study Guide* as their primary text. For more able students, you can use the recommendations for universal access in the Teacher's Edition of your textbook.

Diagnostic Readiness Tests (pages 6–26)

The Diagnostic Readiness Tests measure your students' abilities in skills essential to success in social studies. There are tests in each of the following categories:

- Geographic Literacy
- Visual Analysis
- Critical Thinking and Reading
- Vocabulary
- Writing

Once you have test results, consult the correlation table in this book to locate program resources for instruction and practice in individual skills. Repeat these tests at least once more during the year to gauge student progress and identify skills needing improvement.

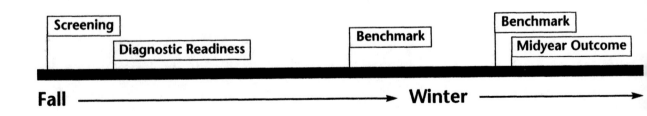

Monitoring Progress Over the Year

The section and chapter assessments in the Student Edition and All-in-One Teaching Resources measure understanding of what students have learned on a short-term basis. To measure student retention over time, it is important to administer Benchmark Tests and refocus instruction based on test results.

Benchmark Tests (pages 39–44, 49–54)

Benchmark testing is at the heart of progress monitoring and student achievement. At specified intervals throughout the year, give Benchmark Tests to evaluate student progress toward mastery of essential content. All questions on the Benchmark Tests correlate to core standards established for this course.

Critical to student achievement is analyzing Benchmark Tests results to adapt your teaching to student needs. Item tallies will show you areas where the whole class is having difficulty and thus merit reteaching. Items with just a few incorrect answers indicate that only certain students need remediation assignments.

Report Sheets (pages 59–62)

The student Benchmark Test report sheet identifies
- test items by number
- correlated standards
- student performance on each test item
- relevant assignments in the *Reading and Note Taking Study Guide* for remediation of items that students have missed.

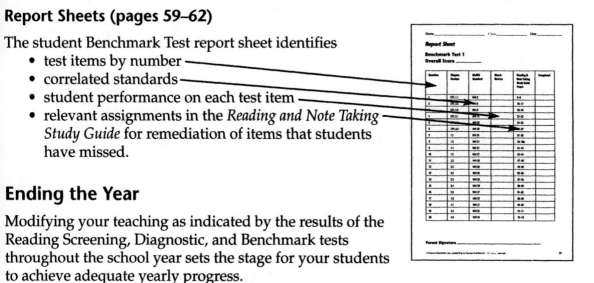

Ending the Year

Modifying your teaching as indicated by the results of the Reading Screening, Diagnostic, and Benchmark tests throughout the school year sets the stage for your students to achieve adequate yearly progress.

Midyear and Final Outcome Tests (pages 45–48, 55–58)

Administer the Outcome Tests to see how well students have mastered course content. Like the Benchmark Tests, Outcome Test items are correlated to course standards.

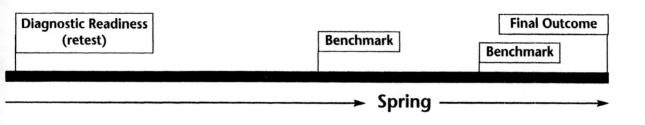

Name _____ Class _____ Date _____

Reading Screening Test

Directions: Read each passage. Then read each question that follows the passage. Decide which is the best answer to each question. Mark the letter for that answer.

---

from *The Professor* by Charlotte Bronte

A FINE October morning succeeded to the foggy evening that had witnessed my first introduction to Crimsworth Hall. I was early up and walking in the large park-like meadow surrounding the house. The autumn sun, rising over the ----shire hills, disclosed a pleasant country; woods brown and mellow varied the fields from which the harvest had been lately carried; a river, gliding between the woods, caught on its surface the somewhat cold gleam of the October sun and sky; at frequent intervals along the banks of the river, tall, cylindrical chimneys, almost like slender round towers, indicated the factories which the trees half concealed; here and there mansions, similar to Crimsworth Hall, occupied agreeable sites on the hill-side; the country wore, on the whole, a cheerful, active, fertile look. Steam, trade, machinery had long banished from it all romance and seclusion. At a distance of five miles, a valley, opening between the low hills, held in its cups the great town of X----. A dense, permanent vapour brooded over this locality—there lay Edward's "Concern."

I forced my eye to scrutinize this prospect, I forced my mind to dwell on it for a time, and when I found that it communicated no pleasurable emotion to my heart—that it stirred in me none of the hopes a man ought to feel, when he sees laid before him the scene of his life's career—I said to myself, "William, you are a rebel against circumstances; you are a fool, and know not what you want; you have chosen trade and you shall be a tradesman. Look!" I continued mentally—"Look at the sooty smoke in that hollow, and know that there is your post! There you cannot dream, you cannot speculate and theorize—there you shall out and work!

---

1. Who is the narrator of this passage?
   - **A** Charlotte Bronte
   - **B** Lord Crimsworth
   - **C** William
   - **D** Edward

2. During which season is the narrator visiting Crimsworth Hall?
   - **A** winter
   - **B** fall
   - **C** spring
   - **D** summer

3. Where is the "great town of X----" in relation to Crimsworth Hall?
   - **A** in a valley five miles away
   - **B** in the woods near the river
   - **C** on the hills of the shire
   - **D** near the newly harvested fields

4. Where will the narrator's new job be?
   - **A** in the town of X----
   - **B** at Crimsworth Hall
   - **C** in the fields collecting the harvest
   - **D** on a river barge

Reading Screening Test *(continued)*

5. In the first paragraph, the narrator observes that the factories "had long banished…all romance and seclusion." What does this imply about his feelings regarding the factories?

   A He admires the technological advancements they represent.

   B He feels intimidated by their size and noise.

   C He feels they have damaged the area's natural charm and beauty.

   D He feels they have improved the area's natural charm and beauty.

6. At the end of the first paragraph, the description of "a dense, permanent vapour" refers to

   A mist rising off the river.

   B steam and smoke from the town's factory.

   C storm clouds that sit on the horizon.

   D morning fog that hides the town from sight.

7. How does the narrator feel about his new job?

   A He is excited by the idea of trying something new.

   B He is grateful for the opportunity.

   C He doesn't have an opinion one way or the other.

   D He feels no enthusiasm for it.

Reading Screening Test *(continued)*

---

from *Brown Wolf* by Jack London

From the thicket-covered hillside came a crashing of underbrush, and then, forty feet above them, on the edge of the sheer wall of rock, appeared a wolf's head and shoulders. His braced forepaws dislodged a pebble, and with sharp-pricked ears and peering eyes he watched the fall of the pebble till it struck at their feet. Then he transferred his gaze and with open mouth laughed down at them.

"You Wolf, you!" and "You blessed Wolf!" the man and woman called out to him. The ears flattened back and down at the sound, and the head seemed to snuggle under the caress of an invisible hand...

In build and coat and brush he was a huge timber-wolf; but the lie was given to his wolf-hood by his color and marking. There the dog unmistakably advertised itself. No wolf was ever colored like him. He was brown, deep brown, red-brown, an orgy of browns. Back and shoulders were a warm brown that paled on the sides and underneath to a yellow that was dingy because of the brown that lingered in it. The white of the throat and paws and the spots over the eyes was dirty because of the persistent and ineradicable brown, while the eyes themselves were twin topazes, golden and brown.

... It had been no easy matter when he first drifted in mysteriously out of nowhere to their little mountain cottage. Footsore and famished, he had killed a rabbit under their very noses and under their very windows, and then crawled away and slept by the spring at the foot of the blackberry bushes. When Walt Irvine went down to inspect the intruder, he was snarled at for his pains, and Madge likewise was snarled at when she went down to present, as a peace-offering, a large pan of bread and milk.

A most unsociable dog he proved to be, resenting all their advances, refusing to let them lay hands on him, menacing them with bared fangs and bristling hair. Nevertheless he remained, sleeping and resting by the spring, and eating the food they gave him after they set it down at a safe distance and retreated. His wretched physical condition explained why he lingered; and when he had recuperated, after several days' sojourn, he disappeared.

And this would have been the end of him, so far as Irvine and his wife were concerned, had not Irvine at that particular time been called away into the northern part of the state. Biding along on the train, near to the line between California and Oregon, he chanced to look out of the window and saw his unsociable guest sliding along the wagon road, brown and wolfish, tired yet tireless, dust-covered and soiled with two hundred miles of travel.

Reading Screening Test (continued)

8. The man and woman in the story live in a cabin
   A in the Oregon mountains.
   B on the Pacific Coast of Oregon.
   C near the California-Mexican border.
   D in the mountains of California.

9. In this story, who is Madge?
   A the man
   B the woman
   C the wolf
   D the dog

10. In the second paragraph, the description of the wolf's head as appearing "to snuggle under the caress of an invisible hand" seems to indicate that the wolf is
    A happy to see the man and woman.
    B afraid of the man and woman.
    C jealous of the man and woman.
    D angry at the man and woman.

11. How does an observer know the wolf is part dog?
    A the shape of its ears
    B the way it barks
    C the way it wags its tail
    D the coloring of its fur

12. Judging by the Irvines' actions in the story, what does their goal seem to be?
    A They want to adopt the wolf as their pet.
    B They want to scare the wolf away from their property.
    C They want to stop it from killing their rabbits.
    D They want to kill it for its fur.

13. What does the narrator's tone imply about his attitude toward the animal?
    A He feels it is dangerous and, therefore, he fears it.
    B He respects it as if it were a superior creature.
    C He feels some affection or admiration for it.
    D He has no feelings for it at all.

Reading Screening Test (continued)

King Kamehameha I of Hawaii

Kamehameha I (1758?–1819) united the Hawaiian islands and then transformed them into a prosperous kingdom that lasted nearly one hundred years. As a young nobleman, Kamehameha readily assessed the threat posed by Europeans and European technology. More importantly, his strength allowed him to preserve his country's independence during the years when his islands were forced open by traders and explorers from Europe and America.

Kamehameha, while not born into Hawaiian royalty, was born into Hawaii's aristocracy. As a result, he received a well-rounded education. A talented student, he seemed to excel at any task set before him, especially those related to war.

British explorer Captain James Cook's visit to the islands in 1778 proved to be an important turning point in Kamehameha's life. As nephew to the Hawaiian king, Kamehameha had the opportunity to meet Cook and his crew and to tour Cook's ship, where he was introduced to the daggers, guns and cannon carried onboard. This experience proved enlightening for the young nobleman, who saw how modern technology made the British nearly invincible. Kamehameha wanted that strength for himself.

He spent the next few years acquiring the military technology he had coveted. He enlisted the help of two British soldiers to teach him not only how to use European weapons, but also how to adapt to Western culture. He then used his knowledge and resources to seize the throne in a ten-year civil war.

Once in power, Kamehameha ruled his kingdom as a feudal monarch. He divided his lands and their inhabitants among his chiefs as a reward for faithful service. He bound others to him by marriage and while he sought the opinions of both foreign and domestic advisors, he kept all decision-making powers for himself.

Under Kamehameha's rule, the islands experienced a much-needed dose of prosperity. This prosperity resulted not only from the stable domestic situation, but also from the establishment of the Hawaiian islands as an important Pacific trade center.

When Kamehameha died in 1819, he left behind a Hawaii very different from the one he had conquered. The islands had become a melting pot. Hardly a ship visited without leaving at least one sailor behind. Native craftsmen, such as blacksmiths and boat builders, had become as skilled in modern methods as their European counterparts.

Even the land itself had been transformed by Kamehameha's policies. The introduction of cattle, sheep, and goats had altered the landscape. Horses, introduced to the islands in 1803, had become a popular mode of transportation and recreation. Foreign vegetables, such as pumpkins, were being grown for export and wild sugar cane was being domesticated.

For 25 years, King Kamehameha had maintained the largest and most stable Polynesian kingdom and he had done so during a period of profound social change.

Name _____ Class _____ Date _____

Reading Screening Test *(continued)*

14. The kingdom established by King Kamehameha lasted almost
  A twenty-five years.
  B two hundred years.
  C one hundred years.
  D ten years.

15. What does the passage imply about the availability of education in old Hawaii?
  A All children received an equal education.
  B Hawaiian children were educated at European mission schools.
  C A well-rounded education was common in Hawaii.
  D Only the upper classes received a good education.

16. What role did Captain Cook play in Kamehameha's life?
  A His visit to Hawaii introduced Kamehameha to the power of European technology.
  B He fought alongside Kamehameha during Hawaii's civil war.
  C He forced Hawaii to trade with Britain.
  D He claimed Hawaii as a British colony.

17. Kamehameha ruled as a feudal monarch. What does that mean?
  A He was both a civil and religious leader.
  B He rewarded loyalty with gifts of land but kept all ruling power for himself.
  C He rewarded loyalty with gifts of land and shared ruling power with his most trusted advisors.
  D He allowed Hawaiian citizens to help him decide important issues.

18. In the seventh paragraph, what is the meaning of the phrase "melting pot"?
  A a piece of cookware
  B a diverse group of people
  C a place for trade
  D a type of prison

19. As a result of Kamehameha's policies,
  A native Hawaiians were able to introduce new technology to the Europeans.
  B Hawaii lost its importance as a trade center.
  C new crops were grown for export.
  D Hawaii became a U.S. state.

20. What seems to be the author's attitude toward King Kamehameha?
  A admiration
  B dislike
  C jealousy
  D love

Diagnostic Readiness Test 1 – Geographic Literacy

Directions: *Use the map below to answer questions 1–4.*

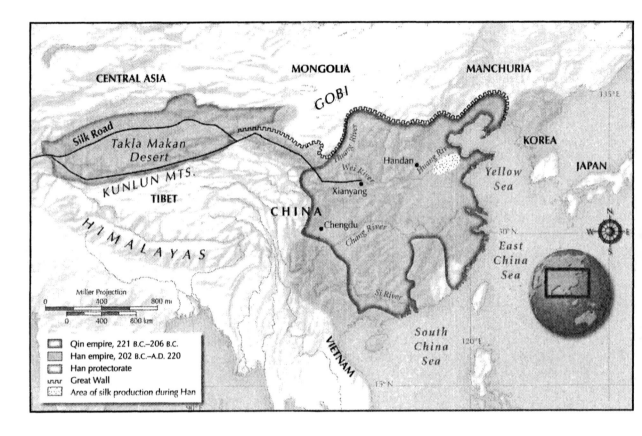

1. According to the map, the Han Empire included
   A Mongolia.
   B Manchuria.
   C Tibet.
   D Korea.

2. China's silk was produced along the
   A Chang River.
   B Huang River.
   C Great Wall.
   D Silk Road.

3. Xianyang marks an endpoint of the
   A Great Wall.
   B Huang River.
   C Silk Road.
   D Chang River.

4. Judging by its location, the Great Wall was built to defend against invasions from
   A Mongolia and Manchuria.
   B Tibet and Central Asia.
   C Tibet and Vietnam.
   D Korea and the South China Sea.

Name _____ Class _____ Date _____

Diagnostic Readiness Test 1 – Geographic Literacy *(continued)*

Directions: Use the map below to answer questions 5–8.

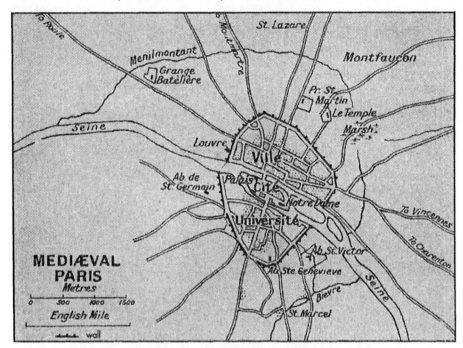

Source: The Perry-Castañeda Map Collection, University of Texas at Austin. Taken from *The Literary and Historical Atlas of Europe* by J. G. Bartholomew, 1912.

5. The river that runs through the city of Paris is called the
   A Montfaucon.
   B Bievre.
   C Seine.
   D Menilmontant.

6. When traveling from Notre Dame to the Louvre, you would most likely pass the
   A Palais.
   B Ab. de St. Germain.
   C Grange Batèlière
   D Ab. Ste. Genevieve.

7. If you leave Paris on the road to Roule, what landmark will you cross once you exit the city walls?
   A the Bievre
   B the Grange Batèlière
   C the Seine
   D the Montfaucon

8. The walled portion of the city is divided into three districts known as
   A Vincennes, Charenton, and Montmartre.
   B Notre Dame, Ab. Ste. Genevieve, and Ab. St. Victor.
   C Louvre, Palais, and Notre Dame.
   D Ville, Cité, and Université.

Name _____ Class _____ Date _____

Diagnostic Readiness Test 1 – Geographic Literacy (continued)

Directions: Use the map below to answer questions 9–12.

9. Which regions of Europe were mainly Roman Catholic?

    A south and east

    B south and west

    C north and central

    D north and east

10. European Muslims lived primarily in

    A the Ottoman Empire.

    B Hungary.

    C Russia.

    D the Holy Roman Empire.

11. If you lived in the city of Moscow, what religion would you most likely practice?

    A Roman Catholicism

    B Anglicanism

    C Lutheranism

    D Orthodox Christianity

12. Explorers from which country would have been most likely to spread Anglicanism?

    A France

    B Spain

    C England

    D the Netherlands

Name _____ Class _____ Date _____

Diagnostic Readiness Test 2 – Visual Analysis

Directions: Use the timeline below to answer questions 1–5.

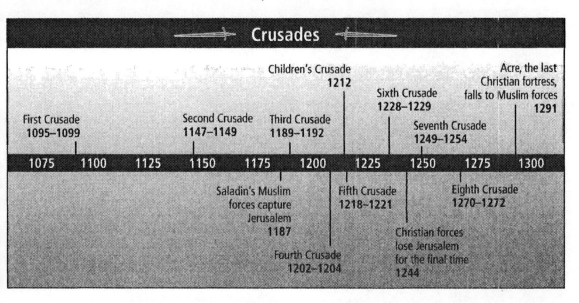

1. How many Crusades were fought in the period covered by this timeline?
   A twelve
   B ten
   C nine
   D eight

2. Which of the Crusades lasted the longest?
   A Seventh
   B Fifth
   C Second
   D First

3. In what year did the last Christian fortress in the Middle East fall?
   A 1291
   B 1272
   C 1244
   D 1187

4. What can be inferred about the motivation for the launch of the Third Crusade?
   A It was to recapture Acre.
   B It was to recapture Jerusalem.
   C It was sent to rescue the Children's Crusade.
   D It was sent to rescue the Second Crusade.

5. What can be inferred about the overall result of the Crusades?
   A They weakened Christianity's influence in Europe.
   B They weakened Muslim influence in the Middle East.
   C They strengthened Christianity's presence in the Middle East.
   D They failed in their objective to claim the Middle East for Christianity.

Diagnostic Readiness Test 2 – Visual Analysis *(continued)*

Directions: Use the image below to answer questions 6–10.

The Ambassadors by Hans Holbein the Younger

6. What does the men's clothing suggest about their social status?

  A They are wearing work clothes, so they belong to one of the lower classes.

  B Their jewelry and hats indicate that they are royalty.

  C Their fancy, elaborate clothes indicate they are men of wealth.

  D They are wearing dark clothing, so they must be priests.

7. This portrait was painted in the year 1533, during the Age of Exploration. How is Europe's interest in exploration reflected in the painting?

  A There are two globes on the shelves and one of the men appears to be holding a telescope.

  B The men's clothing looks like it is more common to Africa or China than to Europe.

  C The tapestry in the painting tells the story of Columbus' journey to the Americas.

  D The rug in the painting is actually a map of the world.

8. The books and instruments are most likely meant to indicate that the men are

  A showing off.

  B trying to sell the items.

  C well-educated.

  D thieves.

9. How does the artist imply that each of these men is trying to be the ideal "Renaissance Man"?

  A He painted the man on the left to look like King Henry VIII of England.

  B He included objects that represent a wide variety of fields such as literature, science and music.

  C He included Greek statues and Roman architecture in the painting.

  D He painted the man on the right to look like Leonardo da Vinci.

10. The object in the middle of the floor is a skull. What does the skull most likely represent?

  A life

  B wealth

  C knowledge

  D death

Name _____ Class _____ Date _____

Diagnostic Readiness Test 2 – Visual Analysis *(continued)*

Directions: Use the chart below to answer questions 11–15.

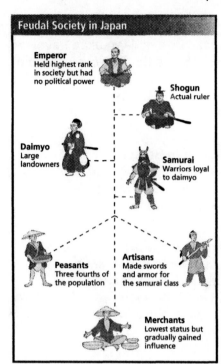

Feudal Society in Japan

Emperor
Held highest rank in society but had no political power

Shogun
Actual ruler

Daimyo
Large landowners

Samurai
Warriors loyal to daimyo

Peasants
Three fourths of the population

Artisans
Made swords and armor for the samurai class

Merchants
Lowest status but gradually gained influence

11. Who occupied the highest position in Japanese feudal society?
   A the shogun
   B the daimyo
   C the samurai
   D the emperor

12. Which group made up the largest portion of the population?
   A the samurai
   B the peasants
   C the daimyo
   D the merchants

13. How does the chart illustrate that merchants had the lowest position in Japanese feudal society?
   A No lines connect them to the peasants or artisans.
   B The merchant in the chart appears to be sitting down rather than standing.
   C They are located at the very bottom of the chart.
   D The merchant wears a different hairstyle than the other figures in the chart.

14. If you were to redraw the chart to illustrate the distribution of actual power, who would be at the top of the chart?
   A the shogun
   B the daimyo
   C the samurai
   D the emperor

15. Why does the chart show no lines connecting the peasants, artisans and merchants?
   A The three groups were at about the same level of society.
   B Each group lived in total isolation and had no contact with the other two.
   C The three groups had only one relationship: with the emperor.
   D The three groups divided ruling power equally among themselves.

Name _____ Class _____ Date _____

Diagnostic Readiness Test 3 – Critical Thinking and Reading

Directions: Read the passage below and answer questions 1–4.

The Great Plague of 1665 was not the first time the disease had wreaked havoc on Britain but it proved to be the worst of the outbreaks. Since the first occurrence of the Black Death in the fourteenth century, the plague had revisited the British Isles on a regular basis. However, even though the population of England had become familiar with the sickness, they still had not deciphered the cause nor had they discovered a cure.

The infection reached the small northern town of Eyam in September 1665 via a package of cloth received by the village tailor. The material, which had been shipped from London, was infested with plague-carrying fleas. The tailor died within four days of obtaining the parcel. Within the next couple of weeks, five more villagers perished.

Up to that point, Eyam's region of the country had not been affected by the epidemic. The village clergyman convinced the townspeople to quarantine themselves so they might save neighboring districts from the ravages of the plague. No one would be allowed to enter or exit Eyam for one full year. Residents of the surrounding area would leave food and other necessities for the sequestered townsfolk at the village limits. Nobody, not even those who lived there, expected Eyam to survive.

At the conclusion of the quarantine year, the first outsiders visited the town, anticipating that they would find everyone dead. Instead, they discovered that more than a quarter of Eyam's population had survived, including some who had intimate contact with diseased individuals.

Every resident of Eyam had been exposed to the plague. Why had some survived untouched when so many others had died? Did the survivors possess a natural immunity?

Modern historians and scientists are working to answer that very question. Using information in the village register, they located descendants of Eyam's plague survivors. By conducting a series of DNA tests on these descendants, researchers hope to identify a genetic trait that establishes immunity to this deadly disease.

1. Why would researchers believe that some residents of Eyam had a natural immunity to the plague?
   A Nobody in Eyam got sick.
   B Survival seemed random.
   C Eyam had a higher survival rate than its neighbors.
   D The plague died out in Eyam earlier than it did in neighboring communities.

2. What would scientists need to find to prove their theory that Eyam's plague survivors had a natural immunity to the disease?
   A plague antibodies in the blood of the survivors' descendants
   B the gene sequence that causes the plague
   C the same genetic marker in the DNA of the survivors' descendants
   D similar white cell counts in the bloodwork of the survivors' descendants

Name _____ Class _____ Date _____

Diagnostic Readiness Test 3 – Critical Thinking and Reading *(continued)*

3. Why might scientists consider Eyam a better subject of study than London or another English city?

   A Eyam's quarantine eliminated the chances of outside influences.

   B The plague in Eyam was worse than anywhere else.

   C Eyam had a greater survival rate than anywhere else.

   D Diaries kept by Eyam's residents give a unique perspective on the plague.

4. Based on the information in the first paragraph, you can infer that

   A the Black Death was worse than the Great Plague.

   B the Great Plague occurred before the Black Death.

   C "the Great Plague" and "the Black Death" are two different diseases.

   D "the Great Plague" and "the Black Death" refer to the same disease.

Diagnostic Readiness Test 3 – Critical Thinking and Reading *(continued)*

Directions: Read the passage below and answer questions 5–8.

Shortly after the establishment of Japan's Yamato dynasty in 500 A.D., the country began importing ideas and technology from its neighbors—specifically China and Korea. From Korea, Japan borrowed weapons, tools, artisans, and scribes. From China, it took Confucianism and a system of writing.

This system of writing, called kanji, is a collection of ideograms, or symbols, that stand for a word. These ideograms, called characters, are then combined to create more complex words. In total, kanji contains approximately 50,000 characters.

To supplement and complement the characters of kanji, the Japanese also invented their own systems of writing, known as hiragana and katakana. These systems contain forty-six kanji characters that have been simplified over centuries of use. These characters include the five vowels used in English, and each of those vowels combined with a consonant.

Once considered "women's writing" because of its rounded, almost cursive appearance, hiragana is used primarily for native Japanese words that have no corresponding Chinese characters. The first writing system taught to Japanese children, it is also used above or next to text in kanji as an indicator of pronunciation.

Katakana, on the other hand, was once considered "man's writing" and is more angular and formal in appearance. Now it is used primarily for words introduced into Japanese from other languages.

5. How many writing systems do Japanese people use?
   A one
   B two
   C three
   D four

6. Which system of writing would you expect to be used in Japanese children's books?
   A kanji
   B hiragana
   C katakana
   D kana

7. In which system of writing would you expect to find the Japanese word for "baseball"?
   A kanji
   B hiragana
   C katakana
   D kana

8. According to the passage, why did the Japanese invent their own systems of writing?
   A They needed new types of writing to express their new spoken language.
   B They wanted their writing to look more European.
   C They wanted their writing to be culturally unique.
   D They wanted to adapt kanji to their own needs.

Name _____ Class _____ Date _____

Diagnostic Readiness Test 3 – Critical Thinking and Reading (continued)

Directions: Read the passage below and answer questions 9–12.

The Peloponnesian War (431–404 B.C.) is often considered the classic example of war between opposite cultures. It was fought between Athens, a democratic society with a trade-based economy and a strong navy, and Sparta, an elitist society with an agricultural economy and a machine-like army.

The war resulted from the spectacular growth of Athens during the 50 years prior to the outbreak of war. With its unrivaled navy, Athens had the potential to totally control trade on the Aegean Sea and disrupt the food supply to the Greek mainland. In response to this threat, Sparta formed an alliance with other Greek city-states, and then declared war on Athens.

Sparta laid siege to Athens in hopes of starving it into submission. However, this strategy had serious flaws. Athens' food supply came not from farmlands surrounding the city but from trade with international allies such as Egypt. Sparta had no control over these food sources. Also, because Sparta was primarily an agricultural culture, its soldiers had to return home every spring and every autumn to tend to their own farms. Athenian soldiers took advantage of these lulls by attacking Sparta's allies.

Despite Athens' seeming advantages, however, it lost the war. The morale of Athenian citizens proved to be too weak to endure a prolonged conflict. The Athenian economy also turned out to be unequal to the task of financing an extended military campaign.

The Spartans, on the other hand, proved themselves to be patient and persistent while they waited for the tide to turn in their favor. That happened with the outbreak of plague in Athens, which weakened the city considerably. Still, the war remained a stalemate for years, until Sparta and its allies were able to establish a blockade around Athens and prevent it from receiving its food supply from abroad. After six months of starvation, the Athenians surrendered and Sparta was victorious.

---

9. Why do you think Sparta formed an alliance before declaring war on Athens?
   A to acquire food to feed its soldiers
   B to hire mercenaries to fight while Spartans tended their farms
   C to borrow money to finance war with Athens
   D to accumulate enough military strength to defeat the Athenian navy

10. Which of the following phrases expresses an opinion?
    A an agricultural economy
    B a trade-based economy
    C a machine-like army
    D a democratic society

11. What does this imply about Athens' citizens that "the morale of Athenian citizens proved to be too weak to endure a prolonged conflict?"
    A They expected a quick victory.
    B They expected to lose the war.
    C They expected a long war.
    D They demonstrated patience.

12. Which of the following was an immediate cause of Athens' decision to surrender?
    A the collapse of Athenian morale
    B the effectiveness of Sparta's blockade
    C the outbreak of plague
    D the decline of Athens' economy

Diagnostic Readiness Test 3 – Critical Thinking and Reading *(continued)*

Directions: Read the passage below and answer questions 13–16.

In Greek mythology, the hero Hercules was required to steal the girdle, or belt, of Hippolyte, queen of the warrior women known as Amazons. The Greek poet Homer also mentions the Amazons in his account of the Trojan War, the *Iliad.*

In all probability, the Amazons of these myths never existed. However, historians and archaeologists do believe that there once was a culture of warrior women in the ancient world, in the steppe region of Russia. The Greek historian Herodotus described these women in his account of a battle along the Thermodon River in present-day Turkey. According to Herodotus' tale, the female warriors lost the battle and were taken away by ship. During the journey, they rebelled and killed the vessel's Greek crew. The ship then drifted across the Black Sea, to the territory of the Scythians. In time, the women intermarried with the Scythians and migrated with them to the Russian steppes. Eventually, they moved farther east to what is now Mongolia.

Archaeologists have uncovered evidence of such warrior women in burial sites on the Russian steppes. This evidence includes females buried in what is considered "attack position" with one leg straight and one leg bent. These women were also buried with weaponry and gold, including arrowheads, gold cups, and gold jewelry.

Now scientists are searching for modern descendants of these ancient warrior women. They believe they have found such descendants in a unique segment of Mongolia's female population that is distinguished by their blonde hair. Geneticists are trying to confirm the genealogy of these women by conducting specialized DNA tests.

13. Why do archaeologists believe that warrior women did exist in the ancient world?

 A Homer wrote about them in the *Iliad.*

 B They found the girdle that Hercules stole from the Amazon queen.

 C They found women who had been buried with weapons and in attack position.

 D They found descendants of the Amazons.

14. What can you infer from the fact that these women were buried with gold objects?

 A They belonged to the lowest class.

 B They were regarded as important.

 C They were hunters.

 D They were religious leaders.

15. Which archaeological find would best confirm Herodotus' account?

 A a Greek ship damaged in battle

 B Greek trade goods buried along the Thermodon River

 C an epic poem that tells of the battle

 D the remains of a fifth century female warrior near the Thermodon River

16. Scientists have found a segment of Mongolia's female population with blonde hair. From this, you can infer that

 A Mongolian women do not usually have blonde hair.

 B Mongolians have blonde hair.

 C Mongolians descend from the Amazons.

 D blonde hair is common among warriors.

Name _____ Class _____ Date _____

Diagnostic Readiness Test 3 – Critical Thinking and Reading *(continued)*

Directions: Read the following passage and answer questions 17–20.

> The Songhai Empire in North Africa broke away from Mali in A.D. 1335. With a skilled army and well-trained cavalry, the new state began to conquer its neighbors. At its peak, the empire stretched from the Sudan in the east to the Senegal River in the west and the desert salt-mines of Teghaza in the north. The empire's wealth came from the Saharan trade in salt and gold, which centered on cities such as Timbuktu.
>
> By the late sixteenth century, the Songhai Empire, having become too large to control effectively, went into decline. Other states began to infringe on the Saharan trade and military invasions soon pushed the Songhai to a limited area along the Niger River. Although the Songhai people were able to keep their own rulers and continue their traditional way of life, their economic and military power had been permanently broken.

17. Where would you be most likely to find modern descendants of the Songhai?

    A in the Sudan

    B along the Nile River

    C along the Niger River

    D in South Africa

18. According to the passage, why did the Songhai Empire start to decline?

    A It was conquered by Mali.

    B It ran out of salt and gold.

    C Its leaders became corrupted by their wealth.

    D It became too large to control effectively.

19. Which of the following groups was most likely to be valued highly in Songhai society?

    A farmers

    B traders

    C storytellers

    D artisans

20. Which word in the second paragraph indicates change?

    A although

    B soon

    C continue

    D having

Name _____ Class _____ Date _____

Directions: Read the following passage and answer questions 21–24.

The first Chinese emperor, Shi Huangdi, began constructing his own tomb as soon as he came to power in 221 B.C. The tomb took 36 years to complete and contains a terra-cotta army of 8000 figures, complete with chariots, weapons, and terra cotta horses. The warriors in this army, which were once painted with bright colors, vary in facial expression and in height. The shortest stand five feet eight inches. The tallest stand six feet five inches.

The first clay soldiers were discovered accidentally in 1974 when Chinese farmers near the city of Shaanxi were digging a well. Subsequent digs revealed that the tomb is divided into four vaults, three of which contain members of the terra cotta army. The soldiers are arranged in a different battle formation in each vault and hold weapons appropriate to the strategy they are displaying. The fourth room remains empty.

In addition to providing examples of ancient Chinese art, these soldiers provide valuable information about Chinese culture and war practices. What they cannot explain is why such a remarkable accomplishment was forgotten for so many centuries.

---

21. What evidence best suggests that Shi Huangdi thought he needed protection in the afterlife?

A The Emperor began building his tomb as soon as he came to power.

B The Emperor had a permanent army buried with him.

C The Emperor made sure he was buried where no one would find him for hundreds of years.

D The Emperor built his tomb as a complex maze so that his body would not be found.

22. Of 1400 warriors in a vault, a few stand a half foot taller than the rest. What is the most logical conclusion regarding the height of the soldiers?

A The taller soldiers held a higher rank in the army.

B The taller soldiers were the chariot drivers.

C The taller soldiers represented those who were the first to die in the Emperor's service.

D The taller soldiers held a lower rank in the army.

23. What evidence best supports the claim that the statues are based on real people?

A Weapons are buried with the statues.

B The number of statues is the same as in a real army.

C The statues are of varied heights and have distinctive facial expressions.

D Bright colors were used to paint the statues.

24. Which of the following statements is the most logical explanation for the empty fourth vault?

A The soldiers that had been in the vault left it to be closer to their friends.

B Shi Huangdi forgot he had built the fourth vault.

C The emperor wanted to have room to grow in the afterlife.

D Shi Huangdi died before his tomb was completed.

Diagnostic Readiness Test 4 – Vocabulary

Directions: Read the passage and answer questions 1–4.

> The Aztec capital of Tenochtitlán covered more than five square miles and supported a population of approximately 400,000, the largest *urban* population in Meso-American history. The center of the city was located on an island in Lake Texcoco and was connected with the mainland by three *causeways*. This portion of the city contained hundreds of temples, including three dedicated to the Aztec gods of war and rain. The Great Temple contained a ball court where the Aztecs played *tlachtli*, and a rack to display the skulls of sacrifice victims. The city had a complex centralized government headquartered in the same palace where the Aztec leader lived. The palace also housed a library and halls of justice. The system was financed by *tribute* paid by the peoples conquered by the Aztecs.

1. An *urban* population is one that
   A lives in the countryside.
   B lives in the city.
   C lives in the suburbs.
   D lives along the coast.

2. A *causeway* is a type of
   A building.
   B temple.
   C bridge.
   D island.

3. Which of the following phrases helps to explain the meaning of *tlachtli*?
   A "a ball court where the Aztecs played"
   B "a rack to display the skulls of sacrifice victims"
   C "dedicated to the Aztec gods"
   D "a library and halls of justice"

4. The Aztecs paid for their city with the tribute they collected. What is *tribute*?
   A human sacrifices
   B honors awarded for bravery
   C blessings granted by the Aztec gods
   D money and goods collected by conquerors

Diagnostic Readiness Test 4 – Vocabulary *(continued)*

Directions: Read the passage and answer questions 5–8.

Babylon's most lasting legacy is the Code of Hammurabi. Not only is the Code one of the earliest examples of a legal system, it is also one of the best-preserved legal systems ever discovered. *Promulgated* by Hammurabi, the sixth king of the Old Babylonian dynasty, the Code contained 282 separate laws. These laws covered a wide range of legal issues including economic, family, civil, and criminal affairs. The Code *meted out* severe punishments for breaking the law. It also established justice according to a system of *retribution*. The laws in the Code combined the legal traditions of two different cultural groups. Therefore, historians assume that the Code was intended to be a universal legal system, used both inside and outside Babylon's borders. Equally significant, the Code did not recognize blood feuds or marriages by capture, both of which had been *condoned* by traditional tribal custom.

5. What word is an antonym for *promulgated*?
   A promoted
   B revoked
   C created
   D advanced

6. In this passage, *meted out* means
   A handed out.
   B abolished.
   C limited.
   D reduced.

7. exoneration: innocence :: retribution: _____
   A revenge
   B forgiveness
   C punishment
   D guilt

8. In this passage, *condoned* means
   A disagreed
   B punished
   C approved
   D rewarded

Diagnostic Readiness Test 4 – Vocabulary *(continued)*

Directions: Read the passage and answer questions 9–12.

In 1492, Columbus sailed the ocean blue, but more than 150 years earlier another explorer made an even more *remarkable* journey. Leaving his home in Tangier in 1325 and returning home in 1354, Ibn Battuta is the only medieval traveler known to have visited the territories of every Muslim ruler of the era. His journeys took him to places as *remote* from each other as China and Spain. In fact, he is estimated to have covered at least 75,000 miles in his travels.

Battuta's *chronicle* of his travels provides rare, *intimate* details about the people and places he encountered. Battuta's reports also reveal a great deal about the political and economic climate of the places he visited. This is especially true in his accounts of the dealings of Muslim traders with their Christian counterparts.

9. What is a synonym for *remarkable*?
   A mediocre
   B common
   C impressive
   D normal

10. In this passage, *remote* means
   A close together.
   B far apart.
   C an electronic control device.
   D easy to get to.

11. The word *chronicle* shares a root with words like *chronic* and *chronological*. This root means
   A study.
   B travel.
   C science.
   D time.

12. In this passage, the word *intimate* means
   A specific and descriptive.
   B plain and generic.
   C very personal.
   D amusing and satirical.

Diagnostic Readiness Test 4 – Vocabulary *(continued)*

Directions: Read the passage and answer questions 13–16.

The Mughal emperor of India, Shah Jahan, so loved his wife that when she died, he wanted to build her a resting place worthy of her beauty and his love. He reviewed plans for her *mausoleum* that had been drawn by architects from all over the Muslim world. Today, the design he chose is known as the Taj Mahal, a *corruption* of his wife's nickname Mumtaz Mahal. The beautiful building remains the *crowning achievement* of Mughal architecture, and took more than 20,000 laborers approximately 22 years to complete. The Taj complex consists of not only a mausoleum of white marble and a mosque of red sandstone but also walls and gardens. The finished *edifice* cost 40 million rupees. Shah Jahan died less than five years after his project was completed. After his death he was entombed in the mausoleum with his beloved wife.

13. In this passage, *mausoleum* means
   A a coffin.
   B a temple.
   C a large tomb.
   D a museum.

14. In this passage, *corruption* means
   A bribery.
   B ignoring illegal activity.
   C a bad habit.
   D a distorted or changed version.

15. A *crowning achievement* is
   A the best or most impressive accomplishment.
   B something that has won many awards.
   C a building established by a king.
   D something that is very expensive.

16. The word *edifice* has a Latin root that means "to build." In this passage, *edifice* means
   A church.
   B structure.
   C tomb.
   D expense.

Name _____ Class _____ Date _____

Diagnostic Readiness Test 5 – Writing: A

Directions: Read the passage. Then complete the assignment below in the space provided.

The Renaissance was a period of great cultural and intellectual accomplishment in Europe. Beginning in Italy in the late fourteenth century and then spreading north through the continent, this period marked a renewed interest in ancient Greece and Rome, in science and technology, and in art and architecture. The achievements of this era include the discovery and exploration of new continents, the invention of the printing press, and the introduction of perspective in painting.

In Italy, the Renaissance focused on the art world. The city of Florence, for example, was home to famous artists such as Michelangelo and Leonardo da Vinci. Da Vinci, in fact, is considered the ideal "Renaissance Man" because of the talent and interest he displayed in so many different fields. His notebooks are filled with ideas for inventions, such as the helicopter, that were well ahead of his time. They also contain sketches that helped him create such notable paintings as the *Mona Lisa*.

In the German states and England, the Renaissance was closely linked with the religious upheaval known as the Protestant Reformation. This northern Renaissance also included significant works of literature by William Shakespeare and Sir Thomas More. Because of the advancements Europeans made during this era, many historians feel that the Renaissance marks the end of the Middle Ages and the start of modern times.

Write one or two paragraphs that express the main idea of this passage. Be sure to include at least three details to support the main idea.

_____

_____

_____

_____

_____

_____

_____

_____

_____

_____

_____

_____

Diagnostic Readiness Test 5 – Writing: B

Directions: Read the passage. Then write a paragraph that answers the following question: What facts are known about the fire in Rome?

Sometime during the night of July 19, A.D. 64, fire broke out near the Circus Maximus, Rome's racetrack. Fire in and of itself was not an unusual summer occurrence in the city, but this blaze proved to be unlike any other. It burned for six days and seven nights before being brought under control. Then it reignited and burned for another three days. By the time firefighters extinguished the flames, two-thirds of Rome had been destroyed.

So how did the fire begin? Most historians believe that the fire resulted from arson. However, the identity of the arsonist continues to be a mystery.

The most popular prime suspect has always been the emperor Nero, who was vacationing outside of Rome when the fire erupted. Once he learned of the blaze, he rushed back to the city and, legend has it, helped with the firefighting efforts. He even opened up his palace to those who had lost their homes, using his own money to provide them with food and shelter.

So why would historians think the emperor ignited the blaze in the first place? His accusers claim that he wanted to rebuild Rome according his own wishes and without the permission or interference of the Senate. These suspicions seem to be confirmed by Nero's actions after the fire, when he bought a number of burned out areas near the Forum and used them as the site of his new Golden Palace.

Nero, however, blamed Rome's Christians for the blaze. The emperor had a long history of persecuting Christians, including a fondness for feeding them to lions during gladiatorial games. A prophecy had spread through the Christian community that Rome would be destroyed by fire as punishment for the emperor's abuses. Some modern historians believe, as Nero did, that the fire was started by someone who hoped to make the prophecy come true.

_____

_____

_____

_____

_____

_____

_____

_____

_____

_____

Name _____ Class _____ Date _____

Diagnostic Readiness Test 5 – Writing: C

Directions: Read the passage below and then write a paragraph answering this question: What caused the outbreak of civil war in England in 1215?

England's King John had accumulated a great deal of debt fighting the Crusades and a war with France. To pay off this debt, John tried increasing taxes, creating new taxes, and taking away the Church's exemption from paying taxes.

Seeing this as an abuse of royal power, England's barons united and, with the help of the Archbishop of Canterbury, compiled a list of demands that would limit the king's authority. This list evolved into the Magna Carta (Great Charter). This document reduced the power of monarchy, established a standardized system of justice, emphasized the rule of law, and protected the rights of free citizens. The charter also prohibited the king from taxing arbitrarily, required just cause for imprisonment, and guaranteed the right to a trial by jury.

At first, John refused to sign the Magna Carta. The barons then demonstrated their power by capturing the city of London. Realizing that he had no other choice if he wanted to keep his throne, John agreed to the barons' terms. He met them at the field of Runnymede on June 15, 1215, and signed the charter into law.

However, John secretly had no intention of obeying the will of the barons. As soon as they left London and returned to their homes, he declared the Magna Carta invalid. The result was a civil war between John and the barons that ended only when the king died of dysentery in October 1216.

_____

_____

_____

_____

_____

_____

_____

_____

_____

_____

_____

_____

_____

_____

Diagnostic Readiness Test 5 – Writing: D

Directions: Read the passage. Then, in your own words, write a two-sentence summary of the passage.

> The teacher Confucius lived during a time of chaos and uncertainty in China's history. He sought to stabilize society by developing a code that would guide people to think and behave in a more civil manner.
>
> Confucius believed that all people possess a natural perfection that is easily corrupted by everyday living. This perfection is best realized by adhering to the notion of *ren*, or human virtue, in one's dealings with others. This means maintaining authority over those in subservient positions, showing obedience to those in superior positions, and giving mutual respect to those of the same social level. By following these guidelines, moral order can be restored and conflict can be prevented.
>
> Confucius believed these guidelines should apply in the political arena, as well, in what he described as "government by virtue." He believed that government members should be chosen on merit, not based on wealth or connections. Confucius' push for such government reforms led to the establishment of China's civil service exam system. That system lasted for nearly 2000 years.

_____

_____

_____

_____

_____

_____

_____

Diagnostic Readiness Correlations	Diagnostic Readiness Test Items	World History
Geographic Literacy		
Using the Cartographer's Tools	Test 1: 1, 2, 3, 4, 5, 6, 7, 8, 9, 10, 11, 12	**SE:** pp. SH28, 5, 7, 9, 15, 17, 31, 33, 35, 41, 42, 51, 70, 81, 85, 92, 100–101, 113, 123, 127, 136, 143, 164, 170, 174, 192, 196, 219, 233, 237, 251, 278, 285, 287, 331, 341, 345, 354, 373, 380, 395, 403, 407, 412, 416, 455, 461, 464, 475, 484, 485, 498, 501, 510, 514, 517, 530, 545, 566, 573, 581, 584, 587, 593, 595, 596, 599, 607, 609, 613, 626–627, 633, 636–637, 649, 653, 660, 665, 671, 676, 679, 684, 694, 698, 705, 712, 721, 728, 735, 737, 739, 745, 749, 755 **TE:** pp. 51, 70, 81, 85, 92, 100–101, 113, 123, 127, 143, 164, 170, 192, 196, 219, 233, 237, 251, 299, 331, 341, 345, 373, 380, 395, 403, 407, 412–413, 431, 435, 437, 442, 455, 461, 464, 475, 501, 510, 514, 545, 566, 573, 581, 584, 587, 599, 607, 609, 626–627, 633, 637, 649, 653, 660, 665, 671, 679, 684, 701, 705, 721, 728, 735, 737, 739, 745, 755 **TR:** Review Unit pp. 11, 14, 43, U1 pp. 14, 33, 34, 54, 55, 75, 76, U2 pp. 12, 32, 33, 52, 70, U3 pp. 13, 35, 75, 76, 95, 96, U4 pp. 14, 15, 35, 36, 56, 57, 77, 78, U5 pp. 15, 34, 35, 53, 54, 73, 74, 94, 95
Analyzing and Interpreting Special Purpose Maps	Test 1: 1, 2, 3, 4, 5, 6, 7, 8, 9, 10, 11, 12	**SE:** pp. SH29, 5, 7, 9, 15, 17, 31, 33, 35, 39, 41, 42, 51, 70, 81, 85, 92, 100–101, 113, 123, 127, 136, 143, 164, 170, 174, 192, 203, 219, 233, 251, 278, 287, 331, 341, 345, 373, 380, 403, 407, 412, 416, 455, 461, 464, 484, 501, 510, 514, 545, 566, 573, 581, 584, 587, 593, 595, 596, 599, 607, 609, 626–627, 633, 660, 665, 676, 679, 684, 694, 698, 701, 705, 712, 721, 728, 735, 737, 739, 745, 749, 755 **TE:** pp. 51, 70, 81, 85, 92, 100–101, 113, 123, 127, 143, 164, 170, 192, 219, 233, 251, 299, 331, 345, 373, 380, 395, 403, 407, 412–413, 431, 435, 437, 442, 455, 461, 464, 501, 510, 514, 545, 566, 573, 581, 584, 587, 599, 607, 609, 626–627, 633, 653, 660, 665, 679, 701, 705, 721, 728, 735, 737, 739, 745, 749, 755 **TR:** Review Unit pp. 11, 14, 43, U3 pp. 80, 83, U4 p. 89

Diagnostic Readiness Correlations	Diagnostic Readiness Test Items	World History
Visual Analysis		
Analyzing Graphic Data	Test 2: 11, 12, 13, 14, 15	SE: pp. SH30, 10, 22, 38, 39, 40, 64, 74, 78, 104, 118, 131, 134–135, 136, 172, 199, 201, 204, 207, 240, 247, 253, 255, 266, 290, 324, 327, 354, 368, 382, 410, 416, 417, 446, 447, 458, 473, 484, 487, 492, 516, 524, 532–533, 535, 543, 544, 555, 556, 567, 572, 576, 585, 591, 597, 599, 606, 610, 646, 655, 660, 672–673, 679, 683, 688, 695, 698, 699, 705, 715, 716, 723, 728, 740–741, 746, 764 TE: pp. 64, 74, 118, 127, 160, 207, 247, 255, 300, 310–311, 327, 368, 426, 458, 487, 492, 533, 535, 543, 544, 555, 567, 572–573, 585, 591, 599, 606, 610, 655, 660, 672–673, 679, 683, 688, 695, 705, 715, 716, 746 TR: Review Unit pp. 29, 37, 40, 43, U2 pp. 17, 20, U4 pp. 82, 85, U5 pp. 39, 42
Analyzing Images	Test 2: 2, 6, 7, 8, 9, 10	**SE:** pp. SH31, 11, 23, 52–53, 57, 58–59, 62, 68–69, 75, 80, 86–87, 88, 96, 97, 103, 106, 107, 117, 122, 126–127, 130, 134–135, 138, 139, 144, 146, 151, 156–157, 159, 167, 172, 177, 185, 190–191, 199, 202–203, 205, 206, 207, 211, 212, 214, 215, 218, 220, 226–227, 229, 231, 242, 243, 252, 261, 262, 269, 273, 274, 277, 278–279, 281, 285, 292, 293, 304, 309, 318, 322, 323, 326, 327, 336, 337, 339, 346, 349, 350–351, 352, 356, 357, 362–363, 366, 368, 370, 372–373, 375, 384, 385, 389, 390, 394, 398, 403, 406–407, 412–413, 414, 418, 456, 462–463, 468, 473, 476, 478, 480–481, 486, 491, 493, 494, 495, 497, 498–499, 504, 518, 519, 523, 524–525, 527, 528, 531, 532–533, 534, 538–539, 547, 548, 551, 570–571, 572–573, 579, 584–585, 589, 598, 605, 609, 611, 615, 618, 619, 628, 632–633, 635, 636–637, 639, 640, 643, 648, 649, 656, 660, 667, 672–673, 674, 678, 679, 685, 694–695, 700, 707, 708, 712, 722–723, 725, 730, 731

Diagnostic Readiness Correlations	Diagnostic Readiness Test Items	World History
Visual Analysis *continued*		
Analyzing Images *continued*		**TE:** pp. 51, 53, 57, 62, 64, 68, 80, 83, 88, 90, 96, 97, 102, 106, 107, 109, 112, 117, 122, 123, 130, 131, 135, 138, 139, 141, 144, 145, 146, 159, 167, 177, 181, 190, 194, 198, 199, 202–203, 206, 207, 209, 211, 214, 220, 226–227, 229, 231, 232, 242, 243, 245, 252, 269, 271, 273, 274, 281, 284, 285, 292, 293, 297, 301, 302, 304, 307, 308, 309, 313, 315, 317, 322, 323, 327, 329, 336, 339, 346, 352, 356, 357, 359, 372, 374, 384, 385, 387, 389, 398, 402, 414, 418, 421, 427, 431, 441, 443, 444, 453, 456, 458, 462, 468, 473, 476, 478, 480–481, 482, 486, 489, 493, 494, 495, 497, 498–499, 518, 519, 521, 523, 527, 528, 531, 533, 539, 548, 553, 561, 564, 566, 575, 579, 587, 598, 603, 610, 611, 618, 619, 625, 632, 635, 637, 639, 640, 641, 642, 648, 649, 651, 667, 672, 678, 681, 683, 696, 700, 703, 707, 712, 716, 725, 730, 731, 733, 740, 747, 767 **TR:** U3 pp. 17, 42, 62
Critcal Thinking and Reading		
Identifying Main Ideas/ Summarizing	Test 3: 5, 8, 17, 18	**SE:** pp. SH4, SH35, SH38, 4, 6, 8, 14, 16, 18, 20, 26, 28, 30, 32, 34, 36, 48, 54, 55, 56, 59, 61, 65, 66, 70, 71, 72, 76, 80, 98, 106, 114, 124, 138, 142, 146, 152, 161, 168, 173, 176, 181, 186, 187, 193, 206, 217, 221, 222, 228, 230, 238, 239, 242, 249, 253, 260, 264, 268, 272, 275, 276, 283, 288, 292, 298, 304, 309, 322, 323, 326, 333, 337, 342, 345, 346, 351, 353, 356, 360, 363, 369, 376, 378, 381, 384, 398, 404, 418, 428, 433, 448, 454, 459, 462, 467, 471, 472, 476, 477, 481, 483, 486, 494, 502, 506, 511, 515, 518, 529, 533, 535, 536, 539, 540, 542, 549, 550, 555, 558, 567, 573, 576, 594, 598, 604, 612, 623, 629, 630, 635, 644, 648, 657, 668, 675, 678, 697, 700, 708, 710, 713, 714, 718, 720, 726, 730, 751, 752 **TE:** pp. 48, 54, 55, 59, 65, 70, 71, 76, 80, 98, 106, 124, 138, 146, 152, 161, 173, 176, 182, 186, 187, 193, 200, 202, 206, 213, 217, 220, 221, 222, 225, 228, 238, 242, 249, 253, 258, 264, 268, 272, 275, 285, 288, 292, 304, 309, 312, 322, 323, 326, 333, 337, 342, 345, 346, 351, 352, 353, 356, 363, 369, 376, 378, 381, 384, 398, 402, 404, 410, 415, 418, 428, 433, 436, 437, 441, 448, 454, 459, 463, 466, 471, 476, 481, 483, 486, 494, 502, 506, 511, 515, 518, 524, 532, 535, 536, 538, 540, 542, 549, 550, 553, 555, 558, 567, 570, 576, 594, 598, 612, 613, 616, 623, 624, 626, 629, 635, 641, 644, 648, 657, 670, 675, 678, 691, 695, 697, 700, 705, 708, 713, 714, 718, 720, 726, 730, 750, 751, 766

Diagnostic Readiness Correlations	Diagnostic Readiness Test Items	World History
Critcal Thinking and Reading *continued*		
Identifying Main Ideas/ Summarizing *continued*		**TR:** Review Unit pp. 8, 11, 14, 16, 40, U1 pp. 2, 3, 4, 5, 6, 8, 11, 12, 22, 23, 24, 25, 42, 43, 44, 45, 46, 63, 64, 65, 66, 67, 73, U2 pp. 2, 3, 4, 6, 21, 22, 23, 24, 41, 42, 43, 44, 60, 61, 62, 64, 65, U3 pp. 2, 3, 4, 5, 17, 21, 22, 23, 24, 25, 43, 44, 45, 46, 63, 64, 65, 66, 67, 84, 85, 86, 87, 93, U4 pp. 2, 3, 4, 5, 6, 8, 23, 24, 25, 26, 27, 44, 45, 46, 47, 48, 50, 65, 66, 67, 68, 69, 74, U5 pp. 2, 3, 4, 5, 6, 8, 23, 24, 25, 26, 43, 44, 45, 50, 62, 63, 64, 65, 82, 83, 84, 85, 86, 89, 93
Sequencing	Test 2: 1, 2, 3, 4, 5	**SE:** pp. SH32, 2–3, 10, 12–13, 22, 24–25, 38, 39, 40, 68–69, 71, 78–79, 104–105, 110, 114, 115, 119, 120, 124, 125, 128, 129, 131, 133, 136–137, 156–157, 174–175, 195, 201, 204–205, 223, 228, 240–241, 266–267, 290–291, 324–325, 330, 333, 334, 337, 338, 342, 343, 346, 348, 353, 354–355, 371, 376, 382–383, 416–417, 438, 446–447, 480–481, 484–485, 491, 508, 510, 516–517, 556–557, 562, 565, 567, 568, 576, 577, 581, 583, 586, 589, 590, 594, 596–597, 646–647, 676–677, 682, 685, 692, 697, 699–700, 728–729, 764–765 **TE:** pp. 68–69, 71, 110, 114, 115, 119, 120, 124, 125, 128, 129, 131, 133, 161, 195, 196, 201, 210, 223, 224, 228, 330, 333, 334, 337, 338, 342, 343, 346, 348, 353, 371, 376, 432, 438, 477, 491, 509, 552, 562, 565, 567, 568, 576, 577, 581, 583, 586, 589, 594, 617, 631, 660, 682, 688, 694, 697 **TR:** Review Unit p. 42, U1 p. 48, U2 pp. 26, 81, U3 p. 27, U4 p. 71, U5 pp. 47, 105
Identifying Cause and Effect/Making Predictions	Test 3: 12	**SE:** pp. SH3, SH36, 59, 76, 78, 80, 84, 89, 90, 93, 94, 95, 98, 99, 101, 103, 106, 114, 128, 138, 144, 160, 167, 170, 176, 186, 193, 206, 210, 215, 227, 228, 234, 237, 240, 242, 246, 249, 250, 253, 254, 258, 266, 268, 275, 280, 281, 287, 304, 309, 322, 356, 384, 388, 391, 392, 398, 400, 404, 405, 409, 411, 413, 415, 418, 422, 428, 429, 433, 434, 438, 439, 445, 448, 459, 465, 471, 473, 483, 484, 490, 493, 494, 496, 502, 505, 507, 511, 512, 515, 516, 518, 535, 540, 549, 555, 556, 558, 566, 567, 568, 576, 583, 594, 598, 629, 644, 648, 652, 657, 658, 661, 662, 668, 670, 675, 678, 685, 700, 708, 718, 719, 730, 739, 757, 761, 763, 766

Diagnostic Readiness Correlations	Diagnostic Readiness Test Items	World History
<td colspan="3">Critcal Thinking and Reading *continued*</td>		
Identifying Cause and Effect/Making Predictions *continued*	Test 3: 12	**TE:** pp. 59, 61, 76, 80, 89, 93, 94, 95, 98, 99, 101, 103, 106, 114, 126, 128, 138, 144, 156, 167, 170, 176, 186, 193, 206, 210, 215, 227, 228, 229, 237, 242, 246, 249, 253, 258, 268, 275, 280, 281, 287, 292, 304, 308, 309, 319, 322, 330, 356, 384, 388, 391, 392, 398, 400, 404, 405, 409, 411, 412, 413, 415, 418, 422, 428, 429, 432, 433, 434, 438, 439, 443, 445, 448, 459, 465, 471, 473, 483, 490, 494, 502, 505, 507, 511, 515, 518, 535, 540, 558, 566, 567, 576, 583, 594, 598, 615, 629, 636, 644, 648, 652, 657, 661, 668, 674, 675, 678, 700, 706, 708, 718, 719, 730, 739, 757, 761, 763, 766 **TR:** Review Unit pp. 8, 18, 32, U1 pp. 27, 32, 38, 41, 51, U2 pp. 8, 20, 46, 50, 68, U3 pp. 29, 65, 72, 89, 92, 102, U4 pp. 19, 22, 29, 30, 33, 51, 54, U5 pp. 11, 28, 102
Making Inferences/Drawing Conclusions	Test 2: 5 Test 3: 1, 2, 3, 4, 6, 7, 9, 11, 13, 14, 15, 16, 19, 20, 21, 22, 23	**SE:** pp. SH35, SH38, 60, 65, 80, 85, 87, 98, 103, 106, 113, 119, 123, 124, 127, 133, 135, 151, 152, 161, 162, 164, 172, 176, 187, 191, 192, 193, 194, 221, 242, 251, 259, 281, 288, 289, 292, 304, 318, 322, 323, 326, 333, 337, 341, 346, 351, 353, 363, 368, 376, 378, 381, 384, 398, 403, 404, 407, 409, 415, 428, 433, 445, 448, 461, 463, 465, 471, 473, 475, 476, 481, 483, 486, 491, 495, 501, 502, 506, 514, 518, 525, 539, 545, 555, 571, 579, 581, 585, 587, 589, 594, 598, 607, 609, 612, 627, 629, 633, 635, 644, 645, 648, 653, 657, 661, 665, 668, 669, 671, 675, 678, 684, 685, 691, 695, 697, 700, 712, 713, 718, 726, 727, 730, 737, 741, 742, 757, 766 **TE:** pp. 60, 65, 85, 87, 98, 106, 113, 119, 123, 124, 133, 135, 151, 152, 162, 164, 172, 176, 187, 191, 192, 193, 194, 200, 221, 242, 251, 259, 281, 288, 289, 292, 299, 302, 304, 311, 317, 318, 322, 323, 326, 333, 337, 341, 346, 351, 353, 363, 368, 376, 378, 381, 384, 398, 403, 404, 407, 409, 415, 425, 428, 433, 437, 444, 445, 448, 461, 463, 465, 471, 473, 475, 476, 481, 483, 486, 491, 495, 501, 502, 506, 514, 525, 539, 545, 555, 571, 579, 581, 585, 587, 589, 594, 598, 607, 609, 612, 626–627, 629, 633, 635, 644, 645, 648, 653, 657, 665, 668, 669, 671, 675, 678, 684, 691, 695, 697, 700, 712, 713, 718, 726, 727, 730, 737, 742, 757, 766 **TR:** Review Unit pp. 4, 5, 6, 7, 20, 32, 33, U1 pp. 21, 28, 29, 30, 49, 53, 59, 62, 70, 74, 83, U2 pp. 9, 11, 29, 40, 51, 66, U3 pp. 8, 10, 11, 12, 17, 30, 32, 39, 42, 44, 80, 100, 102, U4 pp. 9, 12, 22, 31, 34, 40, 43, 51, 53, 54, 85, U5 pp. 9, 13, 30, 31, 32, 49, 52, 72, 91, 92, 102

Diagnostic Readiness Correlations	Diagnostic Readiness Test Items	World History
Making Valid Generalizations	Test 2: 6, 7 Test 3: 1, 16	**SE:** pp. 54, 76, 124, 167, 191, 201, 212, 259, 262, 281, 476, 612, 622, 723 **TE:** pp. 54, 76, 124, 167, 191, 201, 212, 259, 262, 281, 476, 482, 612, 622, 723 **TR:** Review Unit pp. 14, 17, 27, 40, U1 pp. 18, 21, 62, U2 p. 59, U4 p. 64, U5 pp. 78, 81
Distinguishing Fact and Opinion	Test 3: 10	**SE:** pp. SH6, 103, 128, 184, 248, 347, 509, 634, 751 **TE:** pp. 103, 128, 220, 394, 479, 506, **TR:** U2 p. 67, U3 p. 28, U5 pp. 9, 33, 90, 99, 102
Comparing and Contrasting	Test 2: 11, 12, 13 Test 3: 3	**SE:** pp. SH35, 55, 59, 61, 71, 103, 118, 119, 124, 146, 161, 164, 167, 172, 176, 185, 203, 206, 221, 233, 238, 279, 352, 356, 380, 395, 433, 438, 448, 486, 499, 528, 540, 549, 591, 594, 612, 622, 648, 661, 668, 678, 705, 734, 737, 738, 742, 744, 751, 753, 757, 758, 763 **TE:** pp. 55, 59, 61, 71, 103, 118, 119, 124, 146, 149, 155, 161, 167, 169, 172, 176, 185, 203, 206, 215, 221, 233, 238, 262, 279, 313, 323, 352, 356, 380, 395, 433, 435, 438, 448, 486, 499, 528, 540, 548, 549, 594, 595, 612, 622, 648, 661, 668, 678, 705, 734, 737, 742, 751, 753, 757, 763, **TR:** Review Unit pp. 3, 21, 24, 27, 31, 33, 37, 40, U1 pp. 10, 12, 38, 41, 69, 83, U2 pp. 7, 10, 11, 28, 37, 40, 48, 75, 78, U3 pp. 9, 42, 50, 53, 73, 100, 103, U4 pp. 11, 32, 64, 85, U5 pp. 10, 13, 22, 42, 58, 61, 68, 88, 102

Diagnostic Readiness Correlations	Diagnostic Readiness Test Items	World History
Critcal Thinking and Reading *continued*		
Analyzing Primary and Secondary Sources	Test 3: 1, 2, 3, 4	**SE:** pp. SH33, 47, 54, 55, 56, 61, 63, 66, 71, 76, 81, 83, 84, 90, 91, 94, 95, 102, 107, 109, 111, 113, 115, 125, 126–127, 128, 129, 139, 142, 147, 150, 154, 155, 159, 162, 163, 166, 171, 177, 181, 187, 188, 195, 197, 207, 210, 213, 222, 223, 225, 230, 234, 243, 246, 250, 254, 257, 259, 260, 269, 271, 272, 276, 277, 283, 289, 293, 297, 298, 305, 312, 319, 327, 329, 330, 332, 334, 337, 338, 343, 348, 349, 357, 359, 360, 364, 371, 377, 378, 385, 387, 388, 392, 399, 405, 419, 421, 422, 429, 434, 439, 449, 453, 454, 460, 466, 467, 469, 472, 477, 487, 489, 490, 496, 503, 506, 507, 510, 512, 519, 521, 522, 524, 529, 536, 542, 546, 550, 559, 562, 568, 569, 582, 586, 590, 599, 604, 614, 618, 623, 630, 638, 645, 649, 652, 658, 662, 669, 670, 679, 682, 691, 692, 701, 704, 710, 714, 719, 720, 731, 734, 738, 744, 752, 753, 767

TE: pp. 47, 54, 55, 56, 61, 63, 66, 75, 76, 81, 83, 90, 91, 94, 95, 96, 102, 107, 109, 111, 113, 115, 125, 128, 129, 139, 142, 147, 150, 151, 154, 155, 156, 157, 162, 163, 171, 177, 181, 187, 188, 195, 197, 207, 210, 213, 216, 222, 223, 234, 243, 246, 250, 254, 257, 259, 260, 269, 271, 272, 276, 277, 280, 283, 286, 289, 293, 297, 298, 303, 305, 308, 312, 314, 319, 327, 329, 330, 332, 334, 338, 343, 348, 349, 350, 357, 359, 360, 364, 366, 368, 371, 377, 378, 385, 387, 388, 392, 400, 405, 411, 413, 419, 421, 422, 423, 429, 434, 436, 439, 444, 449, 454, 460, 467, 469, 472, 477, 487, 489, 490, 496, 503, 507, 512, 513, 519, 521, 522, 524, 529, 536, 542, 546, 550, 559, 561, 568, 569, 574, 586, 588, 590, 599, 604, 614, 623, 630, 633, 638, 645, 649, 652, 658, 662, 669, 670, 675, 679, 682, 684, 694, 701, 704, 710, 714, 716, 719, 720, 731, 734, 738, 746, 752, 753, 767

TR: Review Unit pp. 5, 7, 17, 18, 19, 20, 24, 27, 30, 31, 33, 34, 44, U1 pp. 13, 28, 29, 31, 49, 51, 71, 73, U2 pp. 8, 27, 67, 69, 82, U3 pp. 8, 31, 32, 50, 51, 74, 93, 94, 107, U4 pp. 10, 34, 73, 75, U5 pp. 48, 49, 91, 106 |
| Recognizing Bias and Propaganda | Test 2: 6 | **SE:** pp. SH6, 64, 91–92, 116, 125, 138, 189, 202–203, 284, 285, 365, 367, 374–375, 378–379, 388, 389, 391, 396, 405, 468, 470, 477, 486, 497, 502, 538–539, 540, 543, 544, 545–546, 553–554, 558, 569, 592, 594, 611, 617, 620, 625, 688

TE: pp. 202–203, 389, 391, 414, 546, 553, 558

TR: Review Unit pp. 14, 20, U1 pp. 31, 50, 52, U2 pp. 27, 31, U3 p. 11, U4 pp. 19, 22, 61, 64, U5 p. 48 |

Diagnostic Readiness Correlations	Diagnostic Readiness Test Items	World History
Critcal Thinking and Reading *continued*		
Identifying Frame of Reference and Point of View	Test 3: 1, 3	**SE:** pp. SH34, 59, 65, 71, 132, 133, 138, 157, 173, 184, 201, 212, 215, 224, 227, 229, 264, 275, 326, 369, 390, 466, 505, 509, 511, 527, 540, 558, 622, 634, 635, 645, 669, 750 **TE:** pp. 59, 65, 71, 73, 102, 116, 121, 133, 138, 157, 165, 166, 173, 183, 184, 185, 189, 198, 199, 201, 212, 215, 219, 220, 227, 229, 231, 257, 264, 265, 307, 326, 336, 369, 379, 390, 394, 402, 425, 427, 442, 461, 466, 504, 505, 509, 511, 527, 530, 540, 553, 558, 565, 611, 622, 635, 645, 653, 669, 688, 694, 750 **TR:** Review Unit pp. 5, 19, 27, U1 pp. 10, 18, 21, 32, 50, 74, U2 pp. 10, 11, 17, 20, 28, 31, 37, 40, 47, 50, 56, 59, 78, U3 pp. 9, 20, 28, 52, 70, 72, 90, U4 11, 32, 43, 52, 55, 72, pp. U5 pp. 10, 13, 29, 50, 51, 58, 61, 68, 71, 89, 99, 102
Decision Making	Test 3: 2	**SE:** pp. SH37, 62, 71, 85, 89, 103, 113, 114, 143, 153, 177, 201, 238, 258, 262, 337, 455, 555, 721, 742, 757 **TE:** pp. 113, 238, 258, 326, 555, 742, 757 **TR:** Review Unit p. 27, U1 pp. 62, 83, U2 pp. 48, 59, 78, U3 pp. 71, 103, U4 pp. 53, 73, 75, 85, U5 pp. 12, 29, 81
Problem Solving	Test 3: 24	**SE:** pp. SH37, 65, 80 **TE:** pp. 342, 563, 754 **TR:** U4 p. 55, U5 p. 61
Vocabulary		
Use Social Studies Terms Correctly	Test 4: 1, 2, 3, 4, 5, 6, 7, 8, 9, 10, 11, 12, 13, 14, 15, 16	**SE:** Social Studies terms are included throughout. Representative pages: pp. SH5, 5, 7, 9, 15, 17, 19, 21, 27, 29, 31, 33, 35, 37, 48, 56, 61, 66 **TE:** Social Studies terms are included throughout. Representative pages: pp. 49, 50, 51, 53, 57, 58, 62, 63, 64, 69, 70, 73, 74 **TR:** Social Studies terms are included throughout. Representative pages: Review Unit pp. 2, 9, 12, 15, 22, 25, 28, 35, 38

Diagnostic Readiness Correlations	Diagnostic Readiness Test Items	World History
Writing		
Identifying Main Ideas	Test 5—Writing: A	**SE:** pp. 80, 93, 98, 103, 106, 124, 138, 167, 176, 193, 264, 268, 318, 353, 356, 369, 391, 445, 465, 494, 515, 540, 583, 629, 726, 737 **TE:** pp. 71, 80, 92, 98, 124, 146, 167, 176, 206, 264, 318, 369, 381, 391, 465, 494, 515, 540, 583, 629, 700, 726, 737 **TR:** U1 p. 41, U2 p. 20, U4 pp. 22, 43, 50
Distinguishing Fact and Opinion	Test 5—Writing: B	**SE:** pp. 80, 93, 128, 146, 201, 228, 258, 268, 275, 304, 322, 333, 337, 342, 391, 398, 404, 742 **TE:** pp. 65, 80, 92, 128, 146, 152, 176, 201, 206, 258, 275, 304, 322, 531, 555, 632 **TR:** U5 p. 9
Identifying Cause and Effect	Test 5—Writing: C	**SE:** pp. 215, 221, 228, 238, 459, 483, 713 **TE:** pp. 215, 221, 228, 242, 459, 465, 483, 486, 713 **TR:** U1 pp. 21, 80, 83, U2 p. 40, U3 pp. 20, 83, U4 pp. 22, 43, U5 pp. 22, 42, 61, 78, 81
Summarizing	Test 5—Writing: D	**SE:** pp. 103, 106, 138, 167, 718 **TE:** pp. 103, 381, 582, 718 **TR:** U1 pp. 21, 80, 83, U2 p. 20, U3 pp. 20, 62, 83, U4 pp. 40, 43, 64, 82, 85, U5 p. 42

Mid-continent Research for Education and Learning
World History Standards (3rd Ed.)

Era 1 — The Beginnings of Human Society

1. Understands the biological and cultural processes that shaped the earliest human communities

2. Understands the processes that contributed to the emergence of agricultural societies around the world

Era 2 — Early Civilizations and the Rise of Pastoral Peoples, 4000–1000 BCE

3. Understands the major characteristics of civilization and the development of civilizations in Mesopotamia, Egypt, and the Indus Valley

4. Understands how agrarian societies spread and new states emerged in the third and second millennia BCE

5. Understands the political, social, and cultural consequences of population movements and militarization in Eurasia in the second millennium BCE

6. Understands major trends in Eurasia and Africa from 4000 to 1000 BCE

Era 3 — Classical Traditions, Major Religions, and Giant Empires, 1000 BCE–300 CE

7. Understands technological and cultural innovation and change from 1000 to 600 BCE

8. Understands how Aegean civilization emerged and how interrelations developed among peoples of the Eastern Mediterranean and Southwest Asia from 600 to 200 BCE

9. Understands how major religious and large-scale empires arose in the Mediterranean Basin, China, and India from 500 BCE to 300 CE

10. Understands how early agrarian civilizations arose in Mesoamerica

11. Understands major global trends from 1000 BCE to 300 CE

Era 4 — Expanding Zones of Exchange and Encounter, 300–1000 CE

12. Understands the Imperial crises and their aftermath in various regions from 300 to 700 CE

13. Understands the causes and consequences of the development of Islamic civilization between the 7th and 10th centuries

14. Understands major developments in East Asia and Southeast Asia in the era of the Tan Dynasty from 600 to 900 CE

15. Understands the political, social, and cultural redefinitions in Europe from 500 to 1000 CE

16. Understands the development of agricultural societies and new states in tropical Africa and Oceania

17. Understands the rise of centers of civilization in Mesoamerica and Andean South America in the 1st millennium CE

18. Understands major global trends from 300 to 1000 CE

Era 5 — Intensified Hemispheric Interactions, 1000–1500 CE

19. Understands the maturation of an interregional system of communication, trade, and cultural exchange during a period of Chinese economic power and Islamic expansion

20. Understands the redefinition of European society and culture from 1000 to 1300 CE

21. Understands the rise of the Mongol Empire and its consequences for Eurasian peoples from 1200 to 1350

22. Understands the growth of states, towns, and trade in Sub-Saharan Africa between the 11th and 15th centuries

23. Understands patterns of crisis and recovery in Afro-Eurasia between 1300 and 1450

24. Understands the expansion of states and civilizations in the Americas between 1000 and 1500

25. Understands major global trends from 1000 to 1500 CE

Era 6 — Global Expansion and Encounter, 1450–1770

26. Understands how the transoceanic interlinking of all major regions of the world between 1450 and 1600 led to global transformations

27. Understands how European society experienced political, economic, and cultural transformations in an age of global intercommunication between 1450 and 1750

28. Understands how large territorial empires dominated much of Eurasia between the 16th and 18th centuries

29. Understands the economic, political, and cultural interrelations among peoples of Africa, Europe, and the Americas between 1500 and 1750

30. Understands transformations in Asian societies in the era of European expansion

31. Understands major global trends from 1450 to 1770

Era 7 — An Age of Revolutions, 1750–1914

32. Understands the causes and consequences of political revolutions in the late 18th and early 19th centuries

33. Understands the causes and consequences of the agricultural and industrial revolutions from 1700 to 1850

34. Understands how Eurasian societies were transformed in an era of global trade and the emergence of European power from 1750 to 1870

35. Understands patterns of nationalism, state-building, and social reform in Europe and the Americas from 1830 to 1914

36. Understands patterns of global change in the era of Western military and economic dominance from 1800 to 1914

37. Understands major global trends from 1750 to 1914

Era 8 — A Half-Century of Crisis and Achievement, 1900–1945

38. Understands reform, revolution, and social change in the world economy of the early 20th century

39. Understands the causes and global consequences of World War I

40. Understands the search for peace and stability throughout the world in the 1920s and 1930s

41. Understands the causes and global consequences of World War II

42. Understands major global trends from 1900 to the end of World War II

Era 9 — The 20th Century since 1945: Promises and Paradoxes

43. Understands how post-World War II reconstruction occurred, new international power relations took shape, and colonial empires broke up

44. Understands the search for community, stability, and peace in an interdependent world

45. Understands major global trends since World War II

World History Across the Eras

46. Understands long-term changes and recurring patterns in world history

Name _____ Class _____ Date _____

Benchmark Test 1

Directions: *Each question is followed by four choices. Identify the letter of the choice that best completes the statement or answers the question.*

1. The earliest civilizations developed near
   A mineral deposits.
   B mountains.
   C rivers.
   D farmland.

2. Athenian democracy is considered limited by modern standards. Why?
   A Only male citizens could participate in government.
   B Only 500 citizens were allowed to participate in government.
   C All male citizens over the age of 30 were expected to participate in the assembly.
   D Members of the Council of 500 were chosen by lot.

3. Romans chose a republican form of government because they wanted to
   A prevent the recurrence of a monarchy.
   B guarantee women a voice in government.
   C limit the power of the emperor.
   D preserve their tradition of religious tolerance.

4. The most powerful force in medieval Europe was
   A the Roman Catholic Church.
   B the manor.
   C the Roman Empire.
   D Hellenistic culture.

5. What is the significance of the Magna Carta?
   A It limited the power of the pope.
   B It allowed the monarch to abolish Parliament.
   C It approved money for wars in France.
   D It asserted that the monarch must obey the law.

6. How did Ivan IV (Ivan the Terrible) shape Russian history?
   A He limited the power of the nobility.
   B He established a tradition for the Russian monarchy of absolute power.
   C He established Moscow as the new capital of the Russian empire.
   D He established Moscow as the center of the Russian Orthodox Church.

7. The development of printing in Europe led to
   A religious tolerance.
   B increased competition with China.
   C increased literacy.
   D increased corruption in the Roman Catholic Church.

Benchmark Test 1 *(continued)*

8. Martin Luther believed that
   A good deeds were necessary for salvation.
   B the pope was the sole religious authority.
   C the Bible should not be translated into the vernacular.
   D salvation could be achieved through faith alone.

9. Why did England's Henry VIII break away from the Catholic Church?
   A He was converted to Protestantism by Martin Luther's teachings.
   B He was angry that the pope refused to annul his marriage to Catherine of Aragon.
   C He was hurt that the pope refused to baptize his son, Edward.
   D He was offended by the formation of the Jesuit order.

10. The most important scientific development during the Renaissance was the
    A introduction of the scientific method.
    B adoption of Chinese acupuncture in medicine.
    C adoption of Egyptian mummification for burials.
    D use of "Arabic" numerals by mathematicians.

11. By the 1500s, the most important element of African trade with Europe was
    A ivory.
    B gold.
    C hides.
    D enslaved Africans.

12. How did the Portuguese gain control of trade in Southeast Asia?
    A They used military force.
    B They established ties with local rulers.
    C They paid money for trading rights.
    D They agreed to share their navigational know-how with local rulers.

13. In the Spanish colonies, power was concentrated in the hands of the
    A peninsulares.
    B conquistadors.
    C creoles.
    D mestizos.

14. Which of the following accurately describes England's American colonies during the 1600s and 1700s?
    A They were granted fewer rights than their Spanish and French counterparts.
    B They enjoyed more self-government than their Spanish and French counterparts.
    C They were politically, economically, and culturally unified.
    D They discovered great riches of gold and silver like the Spanish did.

Benchmark Test 1 *(continued)*

Use the map to answer Question 18.

15. The international trade network that included the Atlantic slave trade was known as
    A the Silk Road.
    B the Columbian Exchange.
    C triangular trade.
    D mercantilism.

16. Expanded trade, an increased money supply, and a push for overseas empires spurred the growth of European
    A communism.
    B absolutism.
    C colonization.
    D capitalism.

17. Among the consequences of England's Glorious Revolution was the establishment of
    A a constitutional government.
    B an absolute monarchy.
    C Parliament.
    D the Commonwealth.

18. According to the map, the only battles that occurred in territory ruled directly by Spain were in
    A the Netherlands.
    B the Ottoman Empire.
    C the English Channel.
    D Spain.

19. Which of the following resulted from the Thirty Years' War?
    A The German states were united.
    B The Netherlands and Switzerland became independent states.
    C The Hapsburgs gained power.
    D France lost territory to Spain and Germany.

20. Which of the following statements describes the result of actions in 1795 by Russia, Austria, and Prussia?
    A Poland became a strong European power.
    B Poland ceased to exist.
    C Poland seized territory from Russia.
    D Poland formed an alliance with Austria.

Benchmark Test 2

Directions: Each question is followed by four choices. Identify the letter of the choice that best completes the statement or answers the question.

1. Which of the following best summarizes the Enlightenment view of women?
   A Women were considered as free and equal as men.
   B Women were expected to participate in public life as equally as men.
   C Women were expected to obtain an education equal to that provided to men.
   D Women were considered to have natural rights to home and family.

2. Catherine the Great is considered an enlightened despot because she
   A expanded Russia's empire.
   B sought to strengthen her power as monarch.
   C instituted reforms such as the abolition of torture.
   D was the only woman of her era to govern a large empire.

3. The Declaration of Independence argues that government should protect the natural rights of the people. This idea was incorporated into
   A the establishment of the U.S. Supreme Court.
   B the charter of the national bank.
   C trade agreements with Britain.
   D the Bill of Rights of the U.S. Constitution.

4. How did the U.S. Constitution reflect the ideas of the Enlightenment thinkers?
   A It focused on art and literature from the Renaissance.
   B It reflected the idea that human beings were corrupted by the evils of society.
   C It established a government free of human restrictions.
   D It viewed government in terms of a social contract.

5. France's revolutionaries followed the example set by leaders of the American Revolution by
   A storming the Bastille.
   B issuing the Declaration of the Rights of Man and Citizen.
   C executing King Louis XVI.
   D initiating the Reign of Terror.

6. How did the Napoleonic Code reverse some of the reforms of the French Revolution?
   A It recognized the peasants' right to lands they had purchased from the Church.
   B It denied women the rights of citizenship.
   C It guaranteed the equality of all citizens before the law.
   D It established women as the recognized heads of households.

7. Which of the following was an unforeseen failure of the Congress of Vienna?
   A The agreements at Vienna influenced European politics for the next century.
   B The agreements at Vienna did not anticipate the effect of nationalism in Europe and Latin America.
   C The agreements at Vienna did nothing to stop Napoleon from escaping exile.
   D The agreements at Vienna prevented large-scale war for nearly 100 years.

8. Which of the following became an important source of power for the Industrial Revolution?
   A steam
   B animals
   C wind
   D nuclear fission

Benchmark Test 2 (continued)

9. Goods could be shipped swiftly and cheaply over land because of the invention of
   A the flying shuttle.
   B the water frame.
   C railroads.
   D horses and carriages.

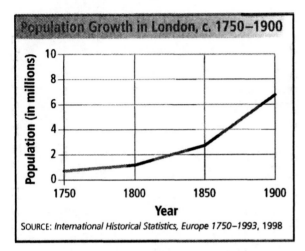

Population Growth in London, c. 1750–1900

SOURCE: *International Historical Statistics, Europe 1750–1993*, 1998

Use the graph to answer Question 10.

10. The type of population growth illustrated in the graph is called
    A urbanization.
    B enclosure.
    C utilitarianism.
    D capitalism.

11. According to Karl Marx, the establishment of a communist society would
    A reverse the capitalist system and make workers the privileged class.
    B create a class struggle between the "haves" and the "have-nots."
    C create the "greatest happiness for the greatest number" of people.
    D end class struggle and distribute wealth and power equally.

12. How did liberalism of the early 1800s reflect Enlightenment ideas?
    A Liberals believed that government should protect the natural rights of individuals.
    B Liberals wanted to restore royal families to their thrones.
    C Liberals wanted to return to life as it was before the French Revolution.
    D Liberals wanted to establish an independent homeland for every nationality.

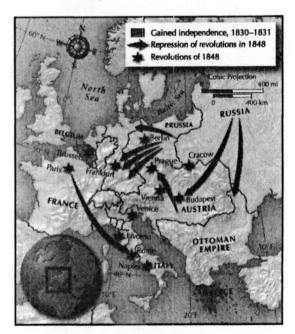

Use the map to answer Question 13.

13. Which newly independent country experienced a revolution in 1848?
    A Italy
    B Prussia
    C Greece
    D Belgium

Benchmark Test 2 *(continued)*

14. Which of the following South American countries experienced the least violent path to independence?
    A Colombia
    B Venezuela
    C Brazil
    D Chile

15. Which of the following was a direct result of the discovery that germs cause disease?
    A the development of anesthesia
    B higher death rates
    C the beginning of nursing
    D improved sanitation

16. "A woman's place is in the home" reflects the values of which of the following groups during the Victorian age?
    A the working class
    B farm workers
    C miners
    D the middle class

17. The romantic movement in art and literature was a reaction against
    A the Enlightenment.
    B nationalism.
    C socialism.
    D Marxism.

18. Which of the following contributed to Germany's growth as an industrial power under Bismarck?
    A tight state control over industry
    B a large overseas empire
    C substantial iron and coal reserves
    D Prussia's victory over the French in the Franco-Prussian War

19. Mazzini, Cavour, and Garibaldi were
    A German socialists.
    B Italian nationalists.
    C Russian communists.
    D Turkish separatists.

20. Which of the following contributed most to the growth of nationalism in the Balkans in the mid-1800s?
    A the decline of the Ottoman empire
    B the spread of democracy
    C the competition between Britain and France for colonies
    D the growing power of Germany

Name _____ Class _____ Date _____

Midyear Outcome Test

Directions: Each question is followed by four choices. Identify the letter of the choice that best completes the statement or answers the question.

1. Which statement correctly describes the Renaissance?
   A It was a time when European countries expanded their borders.
   B It was a period in Europe's history associated with mass migration.
   C It was a time of creativity and political, social, economic, and cultural changes.
   D It was an era synonymous with harsh rulers and economic hardships.

2. How did the printing press affect Europe in the late 1400s and 1500s?
   A Books quickly became collector's items and sold for large sums of money.
   B More people learned to read and gained access to a broad range of knowledge.
   C The printing press provided hundreds of jobs for Chinese pressmen.
   D Outraged rulers banned its use, fearing it would be used to produce propaganda.

3. How was the Protestant Reformation an outgrowth of the Renaissance?
   A Artists used their skills to promote religious revolution.
   B The Renaissance inspired conversions to Greek and Roman religions.
   C Renaissance humanism inspired many people to reshape society.
   D The Renaissance introduced the teachings of Islam to a broader audience.

4. Which of the following best explains why European rulers encouraged ocean exploration?
   A They wanted to find new trade routes.
   B They wanted to conquer new lands.
   C They wanted to spread Islam.
   D They wanted to test new navigational tools.

5. Which statement most accurately compares the trade policies of the Qing in China and the Tokugawa in Japan?
   A The Qing welcomed trade with Europe but the Tokugawa did not.
   B Both the Qing and the Tokugawa welcomed trade with Europe.
   C The Qing rejected trade with Europe but the Tokugawa welcomed it.
   D Both the Qing and the Tokugawa rejected trade with Europe.

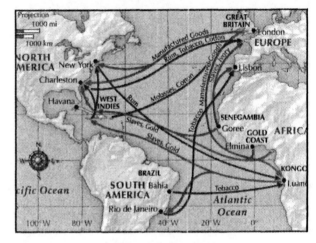

Use the map to answer Question 6.

6. What were slaves exchanged for in Rio de Janeiro?
   A rum
   B tobacco
   C gold
   D molasses

7. Which European monarch described his role as "I am the state"?
   A Louis XIV of France
   B Philip II of Spain
   C Ivan III of Russia
   D Henry IV of France

Midyear Outcome Test *(continued)*

8. During England's Commonwealth of the 1600s, the Puritan government

  A established unconditional freedom of religion.

  B granted equal rights for women.

  C created a constitutional monarchy.

  D encouraged education for all people.

9. The Treaty of Westphalia marked the conclusion of the

  A War of Spanish Succession.

  B Thirty Years' War.

  C English Civil War.

  D Seven Years' War.

10. The separation of powers in the United States government is based on a theory proposed by which philosopher?

  A Socrates

  B Aristotle

  C Montesquieu

  D Locke

11. Both the U.S. Constitution and the Napoleonic Code

  A abolished feudalism.

  B established a meritocracy.

  C guaranteed the equality of all citizens before the law.

  D recognized peasant ownership of land.

12. Why was Napoleon's rule considered democratic despotism?

  A He held plebiscites, but also wielded absolute power.

  B He was elected to power, but then disbanded Parliament.

  C He seized power as a dictator, but then held open elections.

  D Even though he ruled as an emperor, he called himself a democrat.

13. Which group benefited most from the Industrial Revolution?

  A the middle class

  B the working class

  C farmers

  D the nobility

14. Socialists sought to end the poverty and injustice of industrial capitalism by

  A keeping government involvement in workers' rights to a minimum.

  B giving the vote to women and workers.

  C putting factories into the hands of the middle class.

  D putting the means of production into the hands of the people.

15. Which of the following was a goal of nationalists in the early 1800s?

  A to establish a homeland for people with a common heritage

  B to restore power to royal families

  C to accept an established church

  D to tolerate ethnic minorities

16. Most leaders of Latin America's nineteenth-century independence movements belonged to which social class?

  A mulatto

  B mestizo

  C creole

  D peninsulare

Midyear Outcome Test *(continued)*

17. The efficiency of factories improved in the early 1900s with the use of
    A steel machinery.
    B the assembly line.
    C child labor.
    D water power.

18. In response to the harshness of industrial life of the 1800s, many Protestant churches supported the
    A women's suffrage movement.
    B cult of domesticity.
    C germ theory.
    D social gospel.

19. Which statement best summarizes the concept of Realpolitik?
    A Moderation in all things.
    B Treat others as you wish to be treated.
    C All men are created free and equal.
    D Power is more important than principles.

20. Why were the Balkans considered a "powder keg" in the early 1900s?
    A The Ottoman Empire engaged in a war for control of the region.
    B The competing interests of nationalist groups and foreign countries destabilized the region.
    C The countries of the region sought to establish their own colonial empires.
    D Religious differences led to conflicts within the newly independent nations.

Name _____ Class _____ Date _____

Midyear Essays

Directions: On a separate sheet of paper, write a short essay of two or three paragraphs to answer each of the following questions.

1. Historians generally consider the Renaissance to be the start of the modern era. To what extent are they correct?

2. How did contact with Europe affect Africa and the Americas?

3. How did absolutism shape Europe during the sixteenth and seventeenth centuries?

4. How did the ideas of the Enlightenment inspire independence movements around the globe?

5. Using Britain and Germany as your chief examples, explain what conditions are necessary for industrialization to occur.

Name _____ Class _____ Date _____

Benchmark Test 3

Directions: Each question is followed by four choices. Identify the letter of the choice that best completes the statement or answers the question.

Number of Overseas Emigrants from Ireland, 1851–1921*	
1851–1860	1,216,219
1861–1870	818,582
1871–1880	542,703
1881–1890	734,475
1891–1900	461,282
1901–1910	485,461
1911–1921	355,295
Total 1851–1921	**4,614,017**

*Primarily to the United States, Canada, Australia, and New Zealand

SOURCE: Commission on Emigration and Other Population Problems, Dublin, 1954

Use the graph to answer Question 1.

1. Which decade saw the smallest number of emigrants from Ireland?
   A 1911–1921
   B 1901–1910
   C 1891–1900
   D 1871–1880

2. Which of the following was used as a justification for imperialism?
   A genocide
   B Social Darwinism
   C respect for cultural diversity
   D resistance to expansion

3. Western imperialist nations tried to modernize the lands they conquered by
   A adopting the cultural traditions of subject people.
   B imposing Western culture on subject people.
   C encouraging subject people to keep their own traditions.
   D showing no interest in the cultures of subject people.

4. At the Berlin Conference of 1884,
   A African leaders voted on which European countries they wanted to rule their homelands.
   B Germany decided how to divide Africa among the Europeans.
   C Asian leaders urged Europeans to colonize Africa.
   D Europeans decided to colonize Africa and divide it among themselves.

5. Why were the British able to conquer India's vast territory?
   A Britain exploited the diversity of the nation.
   B Most Indians did not speak or write English.
   C India was a vast territory with a small population.
   D The Indian people were attracted to the British way of life.

6. Which of the following was true of Japan under the Tokugawa shogunate?
   A It had good trade relations with the Europeans.
   B It was isolated from the rest of the world.
   C It was a haven for Christians.
   D It was the center of a flourishing Pacific trade.

7. Which Asian countries used modern technological and industrial innovations to successfully prevent takeover by foreign imperialists?
   A Japan and Siam
   B Vietnam and Korea
   C the Philippines and Burma
   D Hawaii and Cambodia

8. The United States intervened in Latin American countries in the early 1900s to
   A spread Western civilization.
   B gain additional colonies.
   C protect U.S. investments.
   D grant independence.

49

Benchmark Test 3 (continued)

9. What led to the assassination of Archduke Francis Ferdinand by a Serbian terrorist and started World War I?

   A A militant Serbian faction viewed Russia as a major political threat.

   B The Serbians viewed the Austrians as foreign oppressors.

   C Serbian nationalists were planning to join Russia.

   D Germany saw the Archduke's planned visit as an outright declaration of war.

10. World War I was more destructive than earlier wars because

    A modern weapons were deadlier.

    B the armies were more ruthless.

    C it lasted longer.

    D airplanes could drop huge bombs.

11. Which of the following statements is true regarding the role of women during World War I?

    A They contributed little to the war effort.

    B Their role during the war differed very little from their peacetime role.

    C They kept their nations' economies going during the war.

    D They focused their efforts on ending the war.

12. The League of Nations might have been more successful if

    A it did not have to compete with the United Nations.

    B the stock market had not crashed.

    C President Wilson had supported it.

    D the United States had joined it.

13. Which of the following was a result of the Bolshevik Revolution?

    A civil war in Russia

    B World War I

    C war between Russia and Japan

    D fighting between the Bolsheviks and the Red Army

14. Lenin's New Economic Policy was designed to

    A end all traces of capitalism.

    B rebuild the Soviet economy.

    C make the Soviet Union into an industrial state.

    D end state control over farms and industry.

15. The main cause of revolution in Mexico in 1910 was

    A high taxes.

    B the unequal distribution of land.

    C a repressive government.

    D food shortages.

16. The Salt March in India is an example of

    A violent resistance.

    B a boycott.

    C civil disobedience.

    D economic sanctions.

Benchmark Test 3 *(continued)*

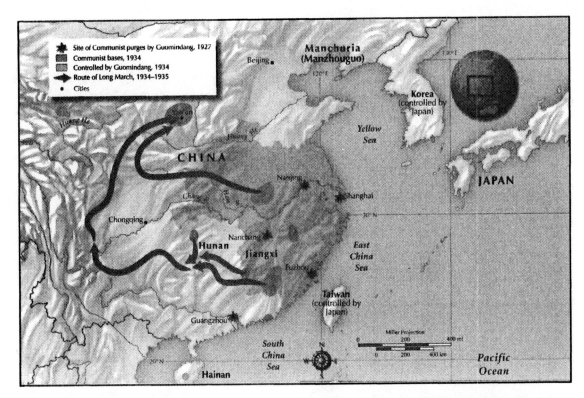

Use the map to answer Question 17.

17. Why might China's Communists have chosen Yan'an as the destination of their Long March?

   A Its location provided the natural protection of the mountains and the Huang River.

   B Its location made cooperation with the Guomindang easier.

   C Its location provided coastal access for trade with their foreign allies.

   D Its location made it easier to defend against the Japanese invasion.

18. One effect of the Great Depression was

   A lower tariffs.

   B an increase in global trade.

   C the spread of democracy.

   D high unemployment.

19. Why did many Italians support fascist, totalitarian rule under Mussolini?

   A It gave most of the governing powers to the people in the lower classes.

   B It eliminated a monopoly of the media, and it imposed strict censorship.

   C It promised a strong government and instilled national pride in Italians.

   D It gave citizens the right to free speech and freedom of assembly.

20. Which of the following is a true statement regarding Soviet society?

   A There were no social classes.

   B Communist party members made up a privileged group.

   C Farm workers made up a new elite.

   D Landowners remained at the top of the social order.

Benchmark Test 4

Directions: Each question is followed by four choices. Identify the letter of the choice that best completes the statement or answers the question.

1. In response to Axis aggression in the 1930s, Western democracies followed a policy of
   A containment.
   B aggression.
   C genocide.
   D appeasement.

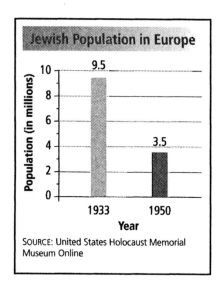

SOURCE: United States Holocaust Memorial Museum Online

Use the graph to answer Question 2

2. The population decline illustrated in the graph is the result of
   A D-Day.
   B the London Blitz.
   C the Holocaust.
   D the bombing of Hiroshima.

3. Toward the end of World War II, Hitler began making mistakes such as
   A underestimating the ability and will of the Soviet Union to fight.
   B launching kamikaze attacks on U.S. ships.
   C fire-bombing Dresden.
   D opening a second front when he invaded Normandy.

4. During the Cold War, the United States reacted to communist expansion efforts by adopting a policy of
   A appeasement.
   B containment.
   C aggression.
   D genocide.

5. Winston Churchill spoke of an "iron curtain" dividing Europe after World War II. To what was Churchill referring?
   A the division of Europe into north and south blocs
   B the struggle for control of Europe's iron resources
   C the re-unification of Germany
   D the division of Europe into Eastern and Western blocs

Benchmark Test 4 *(continued)*

Use the map to answer Question 6.

6. Why might the United States have wanted to attack targets in Cambodia?
   A to establish American military bases closer to North Vietnam
   B to disrupt the Ho Chi Minh Trail supply line
   C to control the Mekong River
   D to secure a buffer zone around Saigon

7. Mao Zedong attempted to increase China's agricultural and industrial output in the late 1950s with the
   A Great Leap Forward.
   B Cultural Revolution.
   C Long March.
   D Pusan Perimeter.

8. The collapse of communism in the Soviet Union resulted in part from Mikhail Gorbachev's policy of
   A containment.
   B collectivization.
   C perestroika.
   D solidarity.

9. Tensions between which two groups resulted in the partition of India in 1947?
   A Hindus and Sikhs
   B Muslims and Hindus
   C Buddhists and Hindus
   D Sikhs and Muslims

10. The Philippines' "people power" revolution unseated Ferdinand Marcos and replaced him with
    A Corazon Aquino.
    B Benigno Aquino.
    C Joseph Estrada.
    D Aung San Suu Kyi.

11. Why did old colonial borders cause problems for new African nations?
    A The borders cut the nations off from important resources.
    B The borders created countries that were too small for their populations.
    C The borders forced together people of different ethnic groups.
    D The borders stopped herders from migrating with their animals.

12. The Middle East is strategically important to the United States because
    A the United States depends on the Suez Canal.
    B the Middle East controls vital oil resources.
    C the United States and the Middle East share religious traditions.
    D the Middle East practices American-style democracy.

13. Which of the following helped end apartheid in South Africa?
    A an oil embargo
    B an international vote
    C economic sanctions
    D a civil war

Benchmark Test 4 (continued)

14. Peace efforts in the Arab-Israeli conflict have been hindered by
   A Arab nations' refusal to recognize Israel's right to exist.
   B Palestinian Arabs' division of Jerusalem into territories.
   C Yasir Arafat's return of the Sinai Peninsula to Egypt.
   D the PLO's refusal to recognize the Golan Heights.

15. In Africa, the spread of drought and deforestation caused
   A an increase in canal building.
   B hunger and migration.
   C rapid population growth.
   D a decline in tropical diseases.

16. Deng Xiaoping expanded China's economy by instituting
   A the Green Revolution.
   B the One-Child Policy.
   C perestroika.
   D the Four Modernizations.

17. Following World War II, what factor led to Japan's economic success?
   A the adoption of an Eastern economic philosophy that emphasized a supply-and-demand economy
   B the concentration on the production of high-quality agricultural products
   C efficient, modern factories adapted to the latest technology
   D a trade agreement with China, the world's largest exporter of goods

18. Germany was able to reunite because
   A Brandt signed a treaty with the Soviet Union.
   B students destroyed the Berlin Wall.
   C communism collapsed in the Soviet Union.
   D the East Germans revolted against the Soviets.

19. The Kyoto Protocol is an effort to
   A achieve global economic equality.
   B protect the global environment.
   C encourage economic growth in underdeveloped nations.
   D stop the spread of AIDS in Africa.

20. Technology has helped form a global culture by
   A spreading ideas rapidly.
   B mass-producing works of art.
   C making all cultures alike.
   D giving all people access to computers.

Name _____ Class _____ Date _____

Final Outcome Test

Directions: Each question is followed by four choices. Identify the letter of the choice that best completes the statement or answers the question.

1. Which of the following contributed to the spread of the Renaissance?
   A the printing press
   B the use of Latin
   C the Protestant Reformation
   D the Catholic Reformation

2. The Italians may have viewed the Renaissance as the rebirth of
   A Minoan civilization.
   B Olmec civilization.
   C Persian civilization.
   D Roman civilization.

3. How did the Napoleonic Code reflect Enlightenment principles?
   A It guaranteed women equal rights.
   B It valued individual rights above all else.
   C It guaranteed the equality of all citizens before the law.
   D It valued the security of the state over individual liberty.

4. The first nations to industrialize were those that had
   A an established middle class.
   B an abundance of natural resources.
   C high tax revenue to use as capital.
   D a diverse labor force.

5. According to Karl Marx, history is determined by
   A individuals.
   B politics.
   C technological innovations.
   D economics.

6. Which of the following goals represents the ideology of nationalists?
   A establishment of a homeland for people with a common heritage
   B restoration of power to royal families
   C acceptance of an established church
   D tolerance for ethnic minorities

7. Which scientific idea of the mid-1800s caused the most controversy?
   A Charles Darwin's theory of natural selection
   B John Dalton's atomic theory
   C Charles Lyell's claim that Earth had formed over millions of years
   D Louis Pasteur's germ theory

8. How did the Industrial Revolution encourage imperialism?
   A It made Europeans feel sorry for their "little brothers."
   B It created a need for land.
   C It created a need for raw materials and markets.
   D It made Westerners feel obligated to improve the human species.

9. To Western imperial powers, modernization meant that subject people should
   A preserve their cultural traditions.
   B accept Western culture.
   C spread non-Western cultures.
   D organize nationalist movements.

Final Outcome Test (continued)

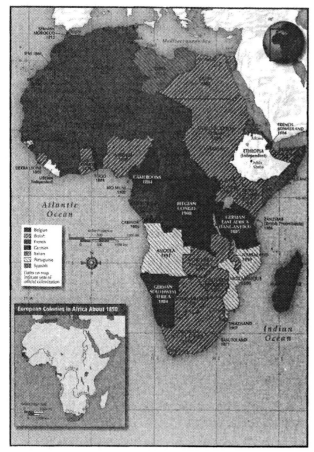

European Colonies in Africa About 1850

Use the map to answer Question 10.

10. The only African nations to preserve their independence during the era of new imperialism were

   A Nigeria and Egypt.

   B Liberia and Ethiopia.

   C Egypt and Angola.

   D Belgian Congo and Ethiopia.

11. Which of the following helped turn World War I into a global war?

   A isolationism

   B the airplane

   C poison gas

   D alliances

12. Which of the following dominated Mexican politics from the 1920s to the year 2000?

   A the Catholic Church

   B the Institutional Revolutionary Party (PRI)

   C the Peronistas

   D the Sandinistas

13. One of Hitler's goals was the

   A persecution and elimination of Jews.

   B continuation of the Weimar Republic.

   C spread of communism throughout the world.

   D creation of a global state.

14. World War II in the Pacific ended with

   A the surrender of Nazi leaders.

   B the bombing of Hiroshima and Nagasaki.

   C the bombing of Pearl Harbor.

   D the invasion of Japan.

15. One of the goals of U.S. general MacArthur's military government in post-World War II Japan was to

   A punish the Japanese people.

   B guarantee democratic government in Japan.

   C restore Japan to its former government.

   D force the Japanese to help rebuild the United States.

Final Outcome Test (continued)

16. The United States' efforts to stop communism during the Cold War led to its involvement in which two "hot" wars?
    A Persian Gulf War and Bosnian Civil War
    B Iran-Iraq War and Persian Gulf War
    C Sri Lankan Civil War and Vietnam War
    D Vietnam War and Korean War

17. Israel refused to give up control of the occupied territories until
    A Arab nations recognized Israel's right to exist.
    B Egypt returned the Sinai Peninsula to Israel.
    C Saddam Hussein was removed from power in Iraq.
    D the PLO surrendered control of Jerusalem.

18. The Chinese government sought to slow excessive population growth by instituting
    A the Long March.
    B the Self-Strengthening Movement.
    C the Kyoto Protocol.
    D the One-Child Policy.

19. Why were the cash economies introduced by the Europeans a failure in some African countries?
    A African countries did not favor international trade.
    B Most people in Africa were subsistence farmers.
    C Africans were not comfortable with interdependence.
    D Africa had no paper money.

Region	Adult Literacy Rate: Males	Adult Literacy Rate: Females	Total Adult Literacy Rate
Sub-Saharan Africa	70	54	62
Arab States	73	51	62
Central Asia	100	99	99
East Asia and the Pacific	95	88	91
South and West Asia	71	45	58
Latin America and the Caribbean	90	88	89
North America and Western Europe	99	99	99
Central and Eastern Europe	99	96	97
World Average	87	77	82

Source: UNESCO Institute for Statistics, March 2004 literacy assessment

Use the table to answer Question 20.

20. Which of the following generalizations about literacy rates is true?
    A There is, generally, a lower literacy rate for females than for males.
    B Females are more likely to go on to higher education than males.
    C Literacy rates in Europe are below the world average.
    D Literacy rates are higher in developing countries than in developed countries.

Final Essays

Directions: On a separate sheet of paper, write a short essay of two or three paragraphs to answer each of the following questions.

1. Were non-European peoples better or worse off as a result of contact with Europe? Explain.

2. What influence has nationalism had on the world since the early nineteenth century?

3. During the period of western industrialization, the economy shifted from agricultural to industrial. How did this change affect the social order?

4. How did the development of communism affect global politics?

5. Do you think that increased global interdependence has led to more cooperation or to more conflict? Explain.

Name _____ Class _____ Date _____

Report Sheet

Benchmark Test 1
Overall Score _____

Question	Chapter, Section	McREL Standard	Needs Review	Reading & Note Taking Study Guide Pages	Completed
1	CPL 1.1	WH 3		8–9	
2	CPL 2.2	WH 8		16–17	
3	CPL 2.3	WH 8		18–19	
4	CPL 3.1	WH 15		22–23	
5	CPL 3.2	WH 20		24–25	
6	CPL 3.3	WH 28		26–27	
7	1.2	WH 31		37–38	
8	1.3	WH 31		39–40	
9	1.4	WH 31		41–42	
10	1.5	WH 27		43–44	
11	2.2	WH 29		47–48	
12	2.3	WH 30		49–50	
13	3.2	WH 29		55–56	
14	3.3	WH 29		57–58	
15	3.4	WH 29		59–60	
16	3.5	WH 27		61–62	
17	4.3	WH 32		68–69	
18	4.1	WH 27		63–65	
19	4.4	WH 32		70–71	
20	4.5	WH 34		72–73	

Parent Signature _____

Name _____ Class _____ Date _____

Report Sheet

Benchmark Test 2
Overall Score _____

Question	Chapter, Section	McREL Standard	Needs Review	Reading & Note Taking Study Guide Pages	Completed
1	5.1	WH 37		74–75	
2	5.2	WH 37		76–77	
3	5.3	WH 32		78–79	
4	5.3	WH 32		78–79	
5	6.2	WH 32		82–84	
6	6.4	WH 32		87–88	
7	6.4	WH 32		87–88	
8	7.1	WH 33		89–90	
9	7.2	WH 33		91–92	
10	7.3	WH 33		93–94	
11	7.4	WH 35		95–97	
12	8.1	WH 37		98–99	
13	8.2	WH 35		100–101	
14	8.3	WH 32		102–103	
15	9.2	WH 37		106–107	
16	9.3	WH 33		108–109	
17	9.4	WH 37		110–111	
18	10.2	WH 35		114–115	
19	10.3	WH 35		116–117	
20	10.4	WH 35		118–119	

Parent Signature _____

Name _____ Class _____ Date _____

Report Sheet

Benchmark Test 3
Overall Score _____

Question	Chapter, Section	McREL Standard	Needs Review	Reading & Note Taking Study Guide Pages	Completed
1	11.2	WH 37		124–125	
2	12.1	WH 37		130–131	
3	12.1	WH 36		130–131	
4	12.2	WH 36		132–133	
5	12.4	WH 36		136–137	
6	13.1	WH 30		140–141	
7	13.1, 13.2	WH 36		140–143	
8	13.4	WH 36		146–147	
9	14.1	WH 39		148–149	
10	14.2	WH 39		150–151	
11	14.3	WH 39		152–153	
12	14.4	WH 39		155–156	
13	14.5	WH 38		157–158	
14	14.5	WH 38		157–158	
15	15.1	WH 35		159–160	
16	15.3	WH 38		163–164	
17	15.4	WH 38		165–166	
18	16.2	WH 42		171–172	
19	16.3	WH 40		173–174	
20	16.4	WH 38		175–176	

Parent Signature _____ Date _____

Name _____ Class _____ Date _____

Report Sheet

Benchmark Test 4
Overall Score _____

Question	Chapter, Section	McREL Standard	Needs Review	Reading & Note Taking Study Guide Pages	Completed
1	17.1	WH 40		179–180	
2	17.2	WH 41		181–182	
3	17.4	WH 41		185–186	
4	17.5	WH 43		187–189	
5	18.1	WH 43		190–191	
6	18.2	WH 43		192–193	
7	18.3	WH 46		194–195	
8	18.5	WH 45		198–199	
9	19.1	WH 43		200–201	
10	19.2	WH 43		202–203	
11	19.3	WH 43		204–205	
12	19.4	WH 43		206–207	
13	20.2	WH 46		210–211	
14	20.3	WH 44		212–213	
15	21.2	WH 45		216–217	
16	21.3	WH 45		218–219	
17	22.1	WH 43		223–224	
18	22.1	WH 43		223–224	
19	22.3	WH 44		227–228	
20	22.3	WH 46		227–228	

Parent Signature _____

Answer Key

Reading Screening Test
Test 1

1. C
2. B
3. A
4. A
5. C
6. B
7. D
8. D
9. B
10. A
11. D
12. A
13. C
14. C
15. D
16. A
17. B
18. B
19. C
20. A

Diagnostic Readiness
Test 1 – Geographic Literacy

1. D
2. B
3. C
4. A
5. C
6. A
7. B
8. D
9. B
10. A
11. D
12. C

Test 2 – Visual Analysis

1. C
2. A
3. A
4. B
5. D
6. C
7. A
8. C

9. B
10. D
11. D
12. B
13. C
14. A
15. A

Test 3 – Critical Thinking & Reading

1. B
2. C
3. A
4. D
5. C
6. B
7. C
8. D
9. D
10. C
11. A
12. B
13. C
14. B
15. D
16. A
17. C
18. D
19. B
20. A
21. B
22. A
23. C
24. D

Test 4 – Vocabulary

1. B
2. C
3. A
4. D
5. B
6. A
7. D
8. C
9. C
10. B
11. D
12. A
13. C

Answer Key (continued)

14. D
15. A
16. B

Test 5 – Writing

A. The student's summary should include all three topics covered in the passage: the characteristics of the Renaissance, the Renaissance in Italy, and the Renaissance in Northern Europe.

B. The student's response should include the following facts: the fire started during the night of July 19, 64 A.D.; the fire burned for a total of 9 days (or 6 days and then reignited and burned for another 3 days); Nero was not in Rome when the fire broke out; Nero bought burned out sections of the city and built a palace there; Nero had a history of persecuting Christians.

C. The student's response should state that the civil war was the result of the barons' efforts to end King John's abuses of power and of John's refusal to obey the Magna Carta.

D. Main idea: Confucius believed that people would get along better if they had rules that told them how to behave in different situations. The guidelines Confucius established became important in Chinese government.

Benchmark Test 1

1. C
2. A
3. A
4. A
5. D
6. B
7. C
8. D
9. B
10. A
11. D
12. C
13. A
14. B
15. C
16. D
17. A
18. A
19. B
20. B

Benchmark Test 2

1. D
2. C
3. D
4. D
5. B
6. B
7. B
8. A
9. C
10. A
11. D
12. A
13. D
14. C
15. D
16. D
17. A
18. C
19. B
20. A

Midyear Outcome Test

1. C
2. B
3. C
4. A
5. D
6. B
7. A
8. D
9. B
10. C
11. C
12. A
13. A
14. D
15. A
16. C
17. B
18. D
19. D
20. B

Answer Key *(continued)*

Midyear Essays

1. Answers should point to the great changes that occurred during the Renaissance, including the shift toward a more global perspective and the development of a more secular, urban society. Student responses may also refer to the expansion of learning and scientific developments of the era, as well as European exploration of the globe, the growth of humanism, the emphasis on trade, and the advancement of the arts.

2. Answers should refer to the effects of the Columbian Exchange including foodstuffs and disease, as well as to the effects of triangular trade. Student responses may also refer to the importation of European culture, politics, and economics to the Americas and to Africa.

3. Answers should refer to the reigns of Philip II in Spain, Louis XIV in France, the Hapsburgs in Austria, the Hohenzollerns in Prussia, and Peter the Great in Russia. Student responses should reference the political and cultural achievements of these rulers, including Peter the Great's Westernization of Russia, the War of Austrian Succession, the building of the palace at Versailles, the development of France's mercantilist policies, Spain's battle for control of the Netherlands, and the defeat of the Spanish Armada.

4. Answers should point to the influence of Enlightenment thinkers on political reforms in England, the incorporation of Enlightenment ideas into the U.S. Declaration of Independence as well as the U.S. Constitution and Bill of Rights, and the inclusion of Enlightenment philosophy in France's Revolution and Napoleon's Code. Answers might also mention how the Enlightenment emphasis on equality and individual rights has been incorporated into modern nationalist and political movements.

5. Answers should point to the need for natural resources, population growth, social mobility, political stability, economic growth, and available capital.

Benchmark Test 3
1. A
2. B
3. B
4. D
5. A
6. B
7. A
8. C
9. B
10. A
11. C
12. D
13. A
14. B
15. B
16. C
17. A
18. D
19. C
20. B

Benchmark Test 4
1. D
2. C
3. A
4. B
5. D
6. B
7. A
8. C
9. B
10. A
11. C
12. B
13. C
14. A
15. B
16. D
17. C
18. C
19. B
20. A

Answer Key *(continued)*

Final Outcome Test

1. A
2. D
3. C
4. B
5. D
6. A
7. A
8. C
9. B
10. B
11. D
12. B
13. A
14. B
15. B
16. D
17. A
18. D
19. B
20. A

Final Essays

1. Answers should suggest that non-European peoples benefited from the education systems and infrastructure-building of imperialist nations but suffered loss of their own cultural traditions and languages, as well as political and economic self-determination. Answers should also refer to the consequences of the Columbian Exchange and the triangular trade. Students could also refer to the cases of Japan and Siam, who selectively borrowed from Europe to make themselves stronger and, therefore, maintain their independence.

2. Answers should suggest that nationalism was the key component in the creation of new nations since the early 1800s, including the unifications of Germany and Italy and the independence movements in Latin America, South Asia, and Africa. Additionally, it has been a factor in the creation of conflict around the world, including the assassination of Archduke Ferdinand to start World War I and modern civil wars in Yugoslavia, Africa, and the Middle East. Nationalism could also be mentioned as a key component of fascism and, therefore, as a cause of World War II.

3. Answers should point to the fact that under the old social order, landowners (the aristocracy) held the highest rank because they controlled the source of food production and the means of survival. The only other social distinction of significance encompassed the peasants who worked the land. As the western world changed from an agricultural economy to an industrial one, the focus switched from land to the manufacturing of material goods as the source of wealth. Those who controlled production became the new elite, and a much more subtle and complex class system emerged based on the types of services people performed in the new industrial society.

4. Answers should suggest that communism was a shaping influence on global politics in the twentieth century. Examples could include the effect of the Russian Revolution on the course of World War I, how the fear of communism contributed to the policies of appeasement of the 1930s, the global consequences of the Cold War, and the effects of the collapse of communism in the Soviet Union and Eastern Europe.

5. Answers supporting the idea of greater cooperation should include the faster spread of ideas, the work of the United Nations, the formation of international economic and environmental treaties, and global scientific and medical cooperation. Answers supporting the idea of greater conflict should include the economic and social disparities between the developed and underdeveloped nations and global conflicts such as the 1970s oil crisis.